Bizarre
Superstitions

thank you

From Elliott

A woman should serve her husband roasted owl if she wants him to be obedient to her every wish.

If you get that "burning" sensation of heat in your ears that occasionally strikes, it means that someone is talking about you: and also, according to some, if your right ear itches, someone is speaking well of you; while if the left one itches, someone is speaking badly of you.

It is better to have your house burn down twice rather than move once.

You do not really understand something unless you can explain it to your grandmother.

When the wolf's ears appear, his body is not far off.

He that fears you present will hate you absent.

A woman's tongue is her sword, and she does not let it rust.

After three days, both fish and guests begin to smell.

He that teaches himself has a fool for a master.

In northern England it was once the custom to toss a plate carrying wedding cake over the bride's head as she left the church. The greater the number of pieces that the plate shattered into, the better the omens for the marriage.

Bizarre Superstitions

The world's wackiest proverbs, rituals, and beliefs

Christopher Cooper

ROBSON
BOOKS

Produced in 2004 by
PRC Publishing
The Chrysalis Building
Bramley Road, London W10 6SP

An imprint of **Chrysalis** Books Group plc

First published in Great Britain in 2004 by
Robson Books
The Chrysalis Building
Bramley Road, London W10 6SP

An imprint of **Chrysalis** Books Group plc

1 2 3 4 5 6 7 8 9

ISBN 1 86105 777 6

Printed and bound in Malaysia

Contents

Introduction

This small book presents an eclectic collection of strange and striking rituals, superstitions, and proverbs. It takes the whole rich tapestry of life as its field of study. Rituals mark the important stages of our lives; proverbs make sense of our shared experience; and superstitions, to a greater or lesser degree, shape the beliefs of the great majority.

Most of us encounter our first ritual early on with our introduction to family, friends, and community through a formal, often religious, naming or baptism ceremony. Further significant stages along life's way are marked by such coming-of-age rituals as the Jewish boy's bar mitzvah, or the Christian child's confirmation. There are rituals to mark the beginning of a marriage, and death rituals to see us into the grave.

In addition to these, most religions have a host of seasonal festivals, with their associated rituals, every year. Believers and nonbelievers alike enjoy the annual celebrations of birthdays and wedding anniversaries, with their own less formally prescribed rituals. The practise and observation of ritual is so important to us that those who cannot accept the rituals of religious faiths often feel driven to invent equivalents of their own ceremonies of infancy, marriage, and death, from which God is absent.

The essence of ritual is that it is *scripted* or *prescribed*. We can detect elements of ritual seeping into everyday life that seem quite informal and spontaneous. When we bump into a neighbor or friend after a lapse of time, we exchange standard greetings and inquiries about how they are and how they've been. We may not be listening too hard to the answers we get back from them, but taking the trouble to go through the ritual of polite conversation is a practical way of showing some goodwill.

More formal rituals come to us ready-made from a distant past. They often contain elements that are completely obscure, but sometimes the meanings of those elements are obvious. A monarch's scepter could be seen as a symbolic club. And it's possible that holding a symbolic club as a sign of the right to rule comes from a distant time when wielding the non-symbolic variety forced others to concede that right.

Obscure or obvious, the elements of a ritual always symbolize some larger reality, often a strangely puzzling one. In this way ritual connects with magic and with superstition. Anyone, no matter how rational, can agree that ritual has important psychological and spiritual functions, such as binding a community together, or keeping alive the memory of the dead. But the participants often believe it can achieve more concrete goals, such as making the rain fall, or helping crops to flourish. Such believers are practicing magic—or, according to the skeptics, indulging in superstition.

Even in Western society, many people would feel distinctly uncomfortable if they didn't knock on wood when they'd expressed some hopeful thought, or didn't cross their fingers on the brink of some wished-for outcome. The less superstitious can also give a nod to these superstitions by using the phrases of these actions, such as "touch wood," or "knock on wood," or "fingers crossed," even if they feel no need to grab at the nearest table or door frame. Only one or two hundred years ago, such charms and spells gave ordinary people a sense of being able to fight back against a powerful, frequently hostile, and little understood universe. No wonder that superstitions still run very deep and live on in otherwise cynical people.

Rest assured, there is often more than one ritual to perform to prevent bad luck occurring. If you don't have any money to turn over in your pocket when you see the new moon, "those that know" might advise you to block out the inevitable bad luck by turning head over heels. But, was this magical remedy devised by some long-forgotten prankster to make fools of generations of the superstitious?

Superstitions are long-lived, and they are frequently adapted to the times. The great folklorist Peter Opie tells how English town-dwelling children adapted a rhyme about counting magpies:

"One for sorrow, two for mirth;
Three for a wedding, four for a birth;
Five for silver, six for gold;
Seven for a secret, not to be told;
Eight for heaven, nine for hell;
And ten for the Devil's own sel [self]."

Since these children did not often see magpies in their urban surroundings, they would take the number on a bus ticket, add the digits together, divide by seven, and apply the rhyme to the remainder. Even in the absence of magpies, they regained the excitement of decoding the mundane events of their lives in terms of a hidden order.

Among those in whom superstition is not immediately obvious, traces usually survive. When we say to someone: "Don't speak too soon," we mean, "Don't tempt fate." We often say such things as: "It was a vacation, so it rained, of course." Behind these phrases is the belief that if we're not careful, "someone out there," most likely fate, is out to get us, and it is the very essence of superstitious belief. "Ill comes often on the back of worse" is a perfect expression of this angst-ridden view of the world.

But traditional superstitions provided not just warnings about the misfortunes brought on us by false steps (such as spilling salt), but also specified remedies (throwing some of the spilled salt over the left shoulder). You can avoid the bad luck that follows when given something sharp, such as scissors or a knife, by giving a small coin in return. This action symbolically turns a gift into a purchase, and the bad luck is fooled or thwarted. Superstitions are not only creators of fear but also dispellers of fear.

There are more nonbelievers today than ever before, yet we seem to need to invent still more superstitions. If a new fountain is built in a park or a shopping mall, passers-by will inevitably throw coins in it and make wishes, just as if it were some ancient spring in a hillside. Chain letters that try to coax money from their recipients, via the internet or conventional mail, often end with a warning that it would be bad luck not to pass the message on, followed by some dire fate that befell someone who didn't. (Which begs the question, how would the sender know this fact?) It's not remarkable that the perpetrator should try to promote the scam in this way but what is remarkable is that many of the chain letter's readers take it seriously and forward the letter as instructed—just in case some evil fate should befall them.

And in addition to these "public" superstitions there are innumerable ones born from personal idiosyncrasies. Sports fans will wear some item of clothing to the game, hoping it will bring luck to the team they support. Entertainers go through sometimes convoluted personal warm-up rituals before they go on stage. Racing drivers will get into their cars a particular way each time they race, and soccer managers have been know to repeat the series of actions they did before a winning game, hoping that it will continue the winning streak. Much of this practice is wrapped in the psychology of positive thinking. If they stick to a routine they believe has previously brought them success then that in turn gives them confidence, and confidence to sports teams can be priceless.

Superstitions in turn contribute a great deal to the subject matter of proverbs, the topic that makes the third main area of interest of this book.

The best surviving proverbs are inevitably pithy and highly memorable. Some are tiny gems of literature—concise, rhythmic, and balanced. Consider for example:

One of these days is none of these days

or

Unminded, unmoaned.

It has been said that a proverb is the embodiment of "the wisdom of many and the wit of one;" and that it consists of "few words, good sense, and a fine image." That successful proverbs embody wit and striking imagery is not in doubt; but the wisdom? If proverbs were wise, they would presumably be consistent, and it's all too easy to find blatantly contradictory proverbs that give wildly different advice.

You can find a proverb to suit almost any mood you wish to express, any inclination you want to justify, or any opinion you wish to defend. Perhaps we can attempt a new proverb to make the point: *proverbs do not convey wisdom unless used wisely*. Or, as a more established one has already expressed it: *Wise men make proverbs, and fools repeat them*.

This book presents many proverbs and also gathers together, in an eclectic way, some of the world's rituals and superstitions. The only criterion of selection was that they should entertain by being in some way fresh and unexpected, not to say downright odd in many cases.

There are many much larger compilations of proverbs, rituals, and superstitions. Some are the lifework of scholars, others the leisure-time hobbies of enthusiastic amateurs. None ever lays claim to being comprehensive, and it is only ever possible to dip into the ocean of strange lore and practise and offer a selection. This collection looks at the weird and wacky side of proverbs and superstitions, focusing on some of the truly baffling things people believe and do, all in the name of luck.

One important disclaimer: I do not believe in a single portent, warning, or charm myself, and none of the descriptions here are meant to be taken seriously. If I break a mirror, I think that it's just my misfortune; I don't think that it's going to bring seven years of bad luck in its wake. Otherwise the men who take the garbage away or work on public refuse sites—who must have broken up a ton of mirrors in their time—must have the worst luck of all. But then again, they haven't got the greatest job in the world, have they?...

Rituals

Birth

All around the world, midwives and the many other birth helpers, have their own magical rituals to ease the pains of labor. These range from ritual fires to flowers, and doing odd things with the placenta.

Labor pains Among the Sia, a native people of New Mexico, the midwife acts out the process of labor. In addition, the father of the woman preparing to give birth burns a ritual fire, dips eagle feathers in the ashes, throws the ashes to the four directions, and then, using the feathers, draws ash down the mother's body. And if that isn't enough, the woman's sister-in-law places an ear of corn near the mother's head, and blows on it during contractions to help the baby out of the body.

Blooming marvels In many cultures, a flower bud is placed in the birth room at the beginning of labor. The heat of the room causes the flower to unfurl, mimicking the arrival of the baby.

Placenta rites The placenta is revered in many societies. Having guarded the baby before birth, it will continue to do so in life. The placenta may be burned or buried with all the ceremony attached to the funeral rites of a person—even as a spiritual mother or sibling to the baby. In the Philippines the placenta is hidden in a bamboo tube and hung in or near the house to guard against evil.

In Bali this reverence is extended to all the accompaniments of birth: placenta, blood, amniotic fluid, and the umbilical cord. They are viewed as the baby's brothers. Before any form of sibling rivalry can occur, the placenta is buried in a small shrine, and prayers are said to it daily.

Death

DISPOSING OF THE DEAD

The Egyptians Several thousand years ago, the Egyptians had developed techniques of preserving, after a fashion, the bodies of the noble or wealthy. Their methods, though crude by modern standards, could be extraordinarily elaborate, depending on the wealth of the deceased. An outline of the most elaborate process is detailed below:

- The first step was to remove the brain of the dead person and to fill the skull cavity with resin.
- Then the internal organs were removed through a hole cut in the abdomen.

They would be washed in spices and either returned to the body or stored in jars that were buried alongside the body.

- The body was immersed in natron (a sodium compound and natural preservative) for up to ten weeks.
- Then the body was cleaned and dried in the sun.
- Over 1,000 yards of bandages were used to wrap the body, before finally it was placed in its sarcophagus.

In Ancient Egypt, the bodies of the dead would be turned round several times after burial, so that the spirits would be confused and could not find their way back to the body or the land of the living to haunt them.

Korean death rites The Korean who dies away from his or her home is traditionally believed to wander forevermore as an unhappy ghost. Therefore, no matter how frail or sick, a person who is believed to be near to death is liable to be dragged home, no matter how far they must go.

After death, hair combed from the head of the corpse and clippings from its nails are gathered and placed in five small wallets, which are interred with the body. Three spoonfuls of rice are inserted into the corpse's mouth, together with coins This rice and money eases the journey of the dead person into the afterlife. The corpse is clad in special cloth and then seven turns of rope are bound tightly around it. Only then is the body ready to be placed in the coffin.

In the past, the oldest male mourner was obliged to spend the entire mourning period lying on a carpet. The period of mourning was typically three days, but for certain classes of people, such as esteemed scholars, it could be longer—in some cases as much as a month. Mourners who had to go outside during the mourning period were obliged to wear a sort of bamboo hat with a wide brim that prevented them from seeing the heavens.

Sitting pretty Among the Native Americans, the Ojibwa buried a dead person in a sitting posture, facing west. Essential articles required for a journey would be placed with the body. After burial, the spirit would stand and begin its westward journey, to the land of the spirits.

Avoiding spirits The Navajo would burn the body of the dead person, as well as his hut. The mourners would take a roundabout route to get home, so that the spirit of the departed person could not follow them. Once home, the friends and relatives would stand in the smoke of a fire to purify themselves.

France In some cultures there is an emphasis on destroying all traces of the dead so that there can be no harmful lingering influence on the world of the living. In France it was once the custom to burn the straw on which a person had lain when dying as well as their clothes (a foresighted precaution to prevent the spread of disease), while neighbors and kin jumped through the flames singing:

Fear, go that way.

Love, come this way.

—words that clearly express the desired outcome of the ritual.

Food for thought Disposing of the dead by burying them in the ground to be corrupted and consumed by worms is a practice that many cultures regard with horror, whereas cremation is viewed as purifying and wholesome. But even this is regarded as wasteful of the precious element of fire by Parsees. They return their dead to the cycle of existence by a more direct route. In Iran and India—even in the heart of the bustling modern city of Benares—stand the Towers of Silence, wooden platforms on which the bodies of the recently deceased are laid, to be consumed by vultures.

Making a snowman Some Inuit (Eskimo) peoples built a small igloo over the body of a dead person, making a sort of snow tomb.

Fat burning In Irian Jaya, which occupies the western half of New Guinea, the Dani people cover a newly dead man's body with pig fat. This makes it burn vigorously in the cremation fire. Arrows are fired into his body to release his spirit to travel to the afterlife. A sacrifice is demanded of a young girl of his family: one joint of a finger, which is hacked off with a stone axe and thrown into the funeral fire. Her loss will be a reminder to everyone of the dead man for as long as she lives.

A dead marriage In Romania, an unmarried woman who dies is traditionally given a "wedding of the dead" on burial, so that her unsatisfied spirit does not return to bother the living. A man plays the role of the groom and takes vows by the coffin. Family and friends play the roles of bridesmaids, and a doll is placed in the coffin to represent the children she didn't have.

Incognito The Tiwi of Bathurst Island, in northern Australia, believe funerals are thronged with evil spirits. The participants at the funeral paint themselves and cut their hair at the ritual so that they go unrecognized.

Never missing a game Certain peoples of Madagascar dig up the bones of the recently dead after the skin has rotted away. While the skin is there, the person's spirit cannot cross to the spirit world. The family wash the bones, and then take them to some favorite event of the deceased, such as a dance or a football game. The bones can be finally returned to the grave, in the knowledge that the spirit has gone to the afterlife. It certainly gives new meaning to the phrase "family outing."

Maoris The Maoris of New Zealand treat the bones of the dead in a similar way. However, they have a distinctive pre-burial ritual. The corpses of the deceased are propped in a sitting position, clad in fine clothes. The whole village views them like this, while mourning and cutting themselves with knives. The hut in which this takes place is later burned.

The great Neanderthal mystery The Neanderthals were either a subspecies of our own species, *Homo sapiens,* or a species closely related to it. They appeared 150,000 years ago, at the same time as the earliest true humans, and disappeared without trace 30,000 years ago, leaving no forwarding address.

Neanderthals buried their dead, but it is a hotly contested question whether this was done ritually. One example of Neanderthal burial has been offered as evidence that they did perform burial rites. At Shanidar Cave in Iraq, there is a Stone-

Age Neanderthal burial near which there are remains of pollen grains and plant stalks. In 1971 the discoverer of the burial suggested that the dead Neanderthal was buried with flowers. Another academic has suggested that these traces were left by the Persian jird, a gerbil-like rodent native to the area, which regularly stores plants in its burrows. But if this is wrong, the fact of a burial ritual would be a striking piece of evidence for a fundamental kinship between the minds of the Neanderthals and those of our own ritual-following species.

Voodoo The voodoo, or Vodun, religion developed in Haiti, first among slaves and then among their descendants, is a blend of African animist religion and Christianity. It believes that the human being consists of at least five different elements, which go their different ways on death. The flesh decays; the spirit passes into the soil; a part called the "star of destiny" represents the fate of the person and goes to dwell among the stars; and then there are two parts of the soul, the *gros-bon-ange* ("great good angel") and the *ti-bon-ange* ("little good angel"). Rituals performed on death are intended to make sure that these components find their way to their proper homes and are not intercepted by sorcerers who can use them to bring harm to the living. One ritual ensures that the *gros-bon-ange* ascends to join the community of ancestral spirits, rather than being trapped on earth. The necessary ritual is expensive, because it requires the sacrifice of an ox or other costly animal; but if it is not performed, the *gros-bon-ange* may cause trouble among the living. A further ritual is performed after nine days, which is the proper time at which the lingering *ti-bon-ange* is released to go to the land of the dead.

Good grief Unrestrained expressions of grief are normal throughout the non-Western world. In Britain, however, for many years it was believed that excessive tears held back the departing soul, and that one should not weep for at least three hours after a death.

THE FINAL HOURS

Certain customs associated with the newly dead were transplanted from northern Ireland to the Appalachians. When a dying person was very close to the moment of death, they would be lifted from the bed to the bare floor. When they had at last expired, the body was laid on a board, a dish of salt mixed with earth was placed on their stomach. All kinfolk and neighbors were obliged to visit, and to touch the corpse. If the corpse began to bleed, the person touching the dead person at the time was suspected of having brought about the death in some way. The dead person was kept at home for a period, while kinfolk sat up with him or her, and prayers and scriptural passages were read. Interestingly, the dish of salt was held to symbolize spirit.

HUMAN SACRIFICE

Aztec gratitude The Aztec civilization of pre-Columbian America was centered around the practice of frequent large-scale human sacrifice. The sides of its pyramidal temples were washed with the blood of the sacrificial victims, who included the most prized among the community's young men and women, or the best specimens among the captured warriors of enemy nations. In this way the Aztec people repaid their debt of gratitude to the sun-god, whose children they believed that they were.

One Aztec rite was devoted to the earth-goddess: the victim was expertly flayed and his skin was worn by the priest. The god of fire, appropriately enough, received his tribute in the form of victims burned alive. The victims sacrificed to the supreme god were prisoners of war, whose living hearts were torn from their bodies.

In one such festival the victim was a prisoner who spent a whole year in preparation. He took the name of the god to whom he was to be sacrificed, and was given four high-born girls as wives. He lived in honor until the day of his sacrifice came, when, at the top of the sacrificial pyramid, a priest tore his heart out.

Great expectations The funeral of the an important or respected person was often accompanied in the past by the sacrifice of others of lower status. In ancient Egypt and China, the wives of a great man who had died, or at least those of them who had not borne children, were killed and buried alongside him, together with rich and rare possessions.

Slave trade In Japan, two or three dozen slaves would be dispatched to accompany some great man in his journey after death.

Suttee In India the practice of *suttee* continued until British rulers outlawed it in the nineteenth century. Traditionally, when a man died, his wife, dressed in her finest clothes, had to mount his funeral pyre and take her place beside him before the torch was put to it.

Marriage

AROUND THE WORLD

Piece of cake In Japan the newly-wed couple cut the wedding cake with a sword.

Plates In northern England it was once the custom to toss a plate that carried a wedding cake over the bride's head as she left the church. The greater the number of pieces that the plate shattered into, the better the omens for the marriage.

Married to debt The wedding ritual sometimes took a strange turn in England in past centuries. It was widely believed that a woman could shake off all her debts if she came to the altar bare foot and wearing nothing but a simple shift. Such a "smock wedding" was, of course, a public humiliation for the groom as much as for the bride, but he may have thought it worthwhile if it enabled him to avoid taking on any liability for her former debts. A variant of this belief was that the husband to be could escape his bride's debts if she walked naked to his home. Whatever the status of these beliefs, they were once so widespread that there is little doubt that they were often acted upon.

Toothy grin In Bali, the bride and groom have their teeth filed at their wedding, by the officiating priest. A person who dies before they are married has his or her teeth filed before the cremation.

Ceremony Among the tribal peoples south of Marrakech, in Morocco, a wedding is usually held a year after the marriage has been agreed between the families of the couple. The ceremony occupies several days. A woman representing the bride's family goes from door to door, a bunch of flowers in her hand, inviting friends and neighbors to come to the wedding. The women of the household beautify the bride with applications of fenugreek and honey and other skin-softening preparations. The bride's hands and feet must be decorated with elaborate designs in henna, which are applied by a woman called the *hennaya*. Traditionally this important task must be carried out by a woman who was the first wife of her husband and herself had never been married before. The ritual of the henna is carried out to the accompaniment of music. Then the bride puts on a white gown. But she must stay in her room until she is taken to her new home. The groom sends a wagon laden with gifts that passes through the streets so that everyone can see the bounty the bride is receiving. Her own family will give her a carpet, dresses, and blankets to equip her house, and, if they are wealthy, her dowry may include a flock of sheep. She will not return to her parents' home for a year, at which time she makes a visit marked by another special ritual.

Indian Ocean A traditional-style marriage ceremony on the island of Madagascar in the Indian Ocean may not be for you, unless you're *very* fond of weddings. A cow is slaughtered during the proceedings and all the guests have to drink its blood.

India Boys and girls of the Gujar caste of India get married at the age of seven. The ceremonies are dedicated to Ganesha, the elephant-headed god. Twice a day for eight days the boy and girl march in procession through the streets. The day before the wedding the boy rides on horseback to his bride's home. He is accompanied by an entourage of 100 friends and relatives, and he is adorned with garlands of bank notes. After the marriage ceremony the bride and groom ride together in a bullock cart to the groom's home, where the bride lives for three days. She then returns to her family and rejoins her husband when she reaches puberty.

Polynesia In the Marquesas Islands in Polynesia, the newly-wed couple depart from the ceremony over a human carpet of the bride's relatives.

Cajuns Among the Cajuns of the southern United States, when a woman is married before her older sisters, those sisters will dance on washtubs at the wedding, while making sweeping actions with their brooms. This little piece of self-mockery highlights to all the eligible men that they are still available.

South Africa In South Africa, the traditional way for the happy couple's families to have fun at the wedding is to sing insulting songs about each other:

> Your son is too poor to marry our daughter.
>
> *or*
>
> You have treated your daughter badly, but now she will be treated like a queen.

Marrying royalty The chance to marry a king is not a hopeless dream in Swaziland. In fact, as many as 20,000 girls dance before him each year, hoping to be chosen as his bride. King Mswati III, the present king, may marry as many women as he chooses; his father, King Sobhuza II, married over 60 women. King Mswati selected brides numbers 11 and 12 in September 2003.

MARRIAGE EN MASSE

Multiple wedding ceremonies are popular in many places, but the world record for marrying in a crowd must surely go to the Rev. Sun Myung Moon's Unification Church, better known as the Moonies. This movement was begun in 1954 by Rev. Moon and is now headquartered in the United States. A key doctrine of the Unification Church is that all humanity possesses Fallen Nature, or Original Sin, because of our descent from Adam and Eve. This will continue until a new Messiah, free of sin, establishes a sin-free family. They believe it was the mission of Jesus to do this, but he failed to marry before his death. However, a second Messiah has been born, in the shape of the Rev. Moon, who received the revelation of his mission from Jesus at Easter in 1936. It is vitally important to the Unification Church that Moon's followers marry among themselves and have children. Accordingly, the Church tells followers whom they should marry, and most comply. The ceremony is both marriage for betrothed couples and a rededication of marriage for those already wed. The five-step Blessing Ceremony consists of the Chastening Ceremony (repentance and forgiveness); the Holy Wine Ceremony (giving grace for what follows); the Holy Blessing Ceremony (spiritual blessing of marriage); the Separation Period (a 40-day period of sexual abstinence); and finally the Three-Day Ceremony (Consummation of the Blessing). The ritual has certainly succeeded: in 1960 the Marriage Blessing was given to three couples in Seoul, Korea; in the following year 33 couples took part; in 1998, it is claimed that 120 million couples took part globally via satellite T.V.

ANIMAL MARRIAGE

Donkeys Sometimes in India a marriage will be arranged between donkeys in the hope that it will bring rain. The ceremony is an ancient one, described in the Hindu scriptures. One such ritual was held in June 2003, at a temple in the city of Bangalore. The bride, called Ganga, wore a green sari, bordered with gold. The groom, called Varuna, wore a white *dhoti,* or loincloth. Guests feasted, and then the donkeys were led in procession through the streets.

Canine nuptials When a child's first tooth appears on the upper gum, the child is believed to be in grave danger. Only marriage to a dog can provide the answer. In June 2003 a nine-year-old girl from the Santhal tribe, West Bengal married a stray dog in an elaborate ceremony. The girl's future marriageability was not adversely affected: she can marry any man of her choice in the future.

Calcutta A similar ritual in 2000 in Kalyani, 30 miles north of Calcutta, was treated with less tolerance by the authorities. After a four-year-old girl was married to a dog to ward off the evil eye, her father was arrested and charged with "a deliberate and malicious act to hurt someone's religious belief;" he was accused of having "damaged Hindu religion."

Pachyderm publicity stunt Two pairs of elephants went through a wedding ceremony in the city of Ayuthaya in Thailand on St. Valentine's Day in 2001. One couple consisted of Sweetheart and Blossoming Lotus; the other two animals were Honey and Golden Tusk. The ceremony, which was held at a department store, was not too serious: its purpose was to publicize Thailand's national animal, the elephant, whose numbers are declining at present.

Religious Festivals

MONDAY BEFORE ASCENSION DAY

The English town of Shaftesbury, Dorset, used to carry out a unique ceremony once a year, originally on the Sunday before Ascension Day, later on the Monday before. The town lies on a hilltop: the little water it had from its wells did not taste as good as that from the neighboring parish of Motcombe. The Mayor would ensure a regular supply of this water by making a gift of local produce to the squire of Motcombe. He would take this, together with a garland of gold and peacock feathers, called the Byzant, in procession to Motcombe. After handing over the produce, the Mayor returned with the Byzant, accompanied by the dancing and carousing people of Shaftesbury, to begin the May festivities. The celebration was discontinued in 1830, being deemed too costly, but has been revived in modern times.

END OF YEAR

One type of old English ritual celebrating the rebirth of the sun after its death in midwinter was the mumming play. The sun was represented by St. George, in shining armor, battling with the "Turkish knight," representing the powers of darkness. However, since dark and light are equally necessary in the scheme of things, a figure called the Doctor would then appear, with a magic potion that revived the slain knight, amid general rejoicing.

Germany There is a game in which a goose is blindfolded and girls make a circle around it. Whoever the goose touches first will be the first to get married.

Ivy can be used to foretell the good or bad fortune of the coming year. For each person whose fate you are interested in, put one green ivy leaf into a bowl of water on New Year's Eve. If it is still green on Twelfth Night Eve, that person will be blessed with good luck. If it has become spotted, it foretells illness. The locations of the spots show the skilled diviner which part of the sufferer's body will be affected by the illness. If the leaf is spotted all over, the victim of the illness will die.

HALLOWEEN

Halloween is said to be derived from the pagan Celtic festival of Samhain, on which the souls of the dead were believed to revisit the earth. "Trick or treat" may be descended from a custom of offering food to the wandering spirits. Nobody is sure when Halloween trick-or-treating began. But as early as October 1917, an observer described a part-Catholic, part-indigenous ritual in a Mexican Indian village in which boys wandered from door to door, singing such chants as:

> Let us pray, let us pray
> We are little angels
> From heaven we come
> If you don't give to us
> Doors and windows we will break!

Leaves can be used to foretell a person's health at Halloween, according to a variant of a similar leaf-divination tradition used at Christmas. Each person places an ivy leaf in a bowl of water overnight. If the leaf bears a coffin-shaped mark the following morning, that person will die within 12 months.

EASTER

Philippines Every Easter, Christ's Passion is reenacted in countless places around the world, mostly those in which Roman Catholic zeal is strongest. The rite at the village of Barangay, in the Philippines, is typical of many. Crowds gather hours beforehand, crowding the narrow streets. Sidewalk vendors sell drinks, barbecued food, and other snacks. The ritual they are waiting to see was established in the 1980s by a local faith healer, and it has flourished despite the disapproval of the Church. A procession of dozens of hooded men with bare backs beat themselves with bamboo sticks, and occasionally are beaten by someone else with a wooden mallet in which are embedded fragments of glass. Sometimes they lie on the ground to receive blows from attendants. Blood spatters the onlookers as the whippings proceed. This part of the festival ends when the flagellants have their wounds dressed, remove their hoods, and stroll home.

England A rather more peaceful custom has long existed in England, and is zealously preserved in some villages today. On Easter Sunday, smartly dressed children form a complete circle around a church, with their backs to the building. They move on to the next church to do the same thing again.

Lifting Another old English custom was that of "lifting," carried out on Easter Monday and clearly related to the Resurrection of Christ. The young men of the locality would lift a chair shoulder-high, bedecked with ribbons and carrying a damsel chosen from among the local girls. They would then carry the chair in procession. The following day it would be the turn of the young women to lift a favored young man in the same way.

The exploding cart One of the strangest of all Easter ceremonies takes place in Florence, in Italy. It is now staged on Easter Sunday, having originally taken place on Easter Saturday. It has been taking place for centuries and commemorates the First Crusade, which culminated in the Christian recapture of Jerusalem in 1099. Stone chips from the Holy Sepulcher were brought back to Florence from Jerusalem, and thereafter were used to strike sparks from which, at every subsequent Easter, holy fires were lit. These were taken to the Cathedral to light the Easter candles, and then were distributed to households, where all fires had been extinguished on Good Friday as part of the Easter observances. At first the fires were carried in a ceremonial cart. This became more elaborate over the centuries. Today it is an elaborate construction built in the seventeenth century, and standing several stories high, and drawn by a team of white oxen garlanded with ribbons. The cart draws up before the Basilica of St. Maria del Fiore of Florence, and a wire is run from the cart to the great altar inside. Now comes the really bizarre part. A firework shaped like a bird and called *la columbina* (the dove), is hung on the wire at the altar, and ignited. The rocket speeds along the wire and hurtles into the cart. The cart's freight consists of a vast number of fireworks of all descriptions, which explode spectacularly. The better the display, the better the next harvest will be.

Eggs is eggs The Easter Bunny works hard at Easter. In Switzerland he puts eggs into nets that children set up in their gardens. In Belgium, too, the traditional hiding place for Easter eggs is in the gardens. The children who search for them, are told that church bells lay the eggs. But in the Tyrol, children collect brightly decorated eggs from neighbors, by going door to door, singing hymns.

Easter eggs do many different jobs in different countries. In Yugoslavia, eggs are dyed black and placed on family graves. Eggs are colored a joyous red in Greece and Romania. When friends meet on Easter Sunday, they knock eggs together, and one cries , "Christ is risen!" while the other responds, "He is truly risen!"

Ukraine In the Ukraine, great effort goes into painting eggs in elaborate designs of personal devising. Stars, suns, triangles, fishes, crosses, and many other objects, all with symbolic meanings, are worked into the designs. The eggs are blessed in church and then eaten at home. To the Ukrainians, the painting of the eggs is of vital importance. Far away, according to tradition, an evil monster is kept in chains. His servants roam the world, counting how many eggs are painted each Easter. If fewer eggs are painted, they can loosen his chains; if more are painted, his chains must be tightened. If one year no eggs should be painted, the monster will be released, and we shall be at his mercy. In the Ukraine they also put painted eggs on graves and cover them with earth. If in the morning the egg is undisturbed, the soul of the dead person is at peace. If the earth has been disturbed, the soul is not at peace and prayers need to said for the deceased.

Pre-Christian Times Eggs have been associated with spring, the season of new birth and awakening, from pre-Christian times. The peoples of the Middle East and of ancient Greece and Rome all exchanged eggs as gifts at their springtime festivals.

Judas beating Easter is a time when effigies of Judas are beaten, hung, and burned in the streets of Mexico. Sometimes in place of the effigy of Christ's betrayer, a decorated container called a *piñata* is beaten with sticks. It is filled with candies, which eventually spill out when it breaks open at the feet of the children.

Roast lamb A common name for Christ is "the lamb of God." A lamb carrying a Christian banner features in many Christian paintings and stained-glass windows. It is therefore of great symbolic meaning that the traditional dish that ends the Lenten fast is roast lamb. In Greece, lamb is traditionally roasted on a spit in villages all around the country. The stomach of the lamb was used to make a soccer ball in the days when the real thing was a scarce luxury, and even the bones of the lamb could be used in children's games.

Paganism

THIASOS OLYMPIKOS

Among the many modern groups that have revived supposedly pagan practices are some devoted to reviving the rituals of ancient Greece. *Thiasos Olympikos* is:

> ...a Religious Association organized for the purposes of facilitating: the honoring of the Hellenic Deities; specifically the Twelve of Olympus, but not limited to Them and specifically including Others: the study and practice of Hellenic and Neo-Hellenic mysticism, and the gnosis [wisdom or spiritual knowledge] derived from that study and practice: the culture surrounding and growing from and related to such.

There is a formal and elaborate set of instructions for the carrying out of rituals for a wide range of circumstances, including frequent festivals in honor of the old Greek gods. The structure of a ritual is prescribed, including the Gathering, the Procession and proceeding to the First Libation (ritual drinking), the Hymn and through to the Final Libation.

The instructions respect modern sensibilities. The Sacrifice is limited to foodstuffs. After the sacrifice, it is explained that:

> At this point it is appropriate for there to be some form of ritual reply from the Deity. It may be that the Deity will take care of this; but it is well to have on hand some formalized version of ritual reply in case the reply from the Deity is not obvious.

The phase of the ritual that follows then is called the Agon:

> In Ancient Times this would be the place for the Sacrificial Dances, such dances filling the time while the priests cut up the sacrificial animal and put the appropriate choice parts upon the sacrificial fire...

> Music and Dancing, immediately following the ritual response, are most appropriate. So are Sacred Games. This is also the place where one might question the Pythoness [a priestess], perform a Healing, perform a Marriage, conduct a funeral, or any number of other activities.

The important thing to remember is that any activity which occupies this place in time is occurring in Sacred Space and Sacred Time. The Agon, like the rest of the ritual, is outside of time and space; between the worlds. This is the place of Sacred Rock and Roll and Sacred Roller Skating and Sacred Trampoline Bouncing. Whatever is done here is done for the Deity, and that focus must be maintained.

THE LUPERCALIA

On February 15, the Romans would mark a festival called Lupercalia, so ancient that no one could remember who it celebrated. It survived until it was abolished by the Christians in A.D. 494. Priests would gather at the cave where, according to myth, Romulus and Remus, the founders of Rome, were suckled by a she-wolf. They would sacrifice goats and dogs, and smear their blood onto the foreheads of two selected youths. Then other priests would wipe the youths clean with wool soaked in goats' milk. The youths and other participants would have to burst into unrestrained laughter at this point, because laughter was especially sacred to Jupiter (another name for Jupiter is "Jove," and joviality takes its name from this.) After everyone had feasted, boys, priests, and other officials ran around what had been the original perimeter of the city, dressed only in loincloths fashioned from the skins of the sacrificed goats. They would lash onlookers with strips of the goatskin, an act that would bring good luck to any person who was struck in this way, and would especially promote fertility and easy childbirth for women.

It was at the Lupercalia of 44 B.C. that Julius Caesar made a fatal mistake that helped to bring about his assassination a month later. Mark Anthony, after taking part in the ceremony, twice offered Caesar a royal crown. Caesar turned it down, apparently because he judged the mood of the crowd to be hostile to giving him this power, but it was felt that he had been too slow to do so. On the Ides of March (March 15), Julius Caesar was murdered in the Senate by conspirators.

MIDSUMMER FESTIVALS

Hot luck Festivals of fire are held at midsummer in many cultures. One ritual involves sending a blazing wheel coursing downhill. It is said to represent the sun's descent in the sky from its highest point at the summer solstice to its lowest at the winter solstice. It is believed that it is good luck if the wheel keeps burning all the way down, but if the fire goes out before the wheel reaches the bottom of the hill, a bad harvest is presaged.

Roast meat In many European countries, cattle and pigs were traditionally put through a sort of ordeal by fire at midsummer, and were driven through flames. This purified them of harmful influences and ensured that they would be healthy and fertile in the coming season.

Fire People, too, have gone through fire rituals that seem to be memories of what would have been terrible ordeals in earlier societies. People would jump over the bonfires, jumping as high as they could to promote the health of the crops. In North Africa childless couples would jump the fires so that they would have children; but in France women early in pregnancy would do so in order to ease their labor. In Ireland and elsewhere unmarried girls would jump the fires to guarantee that they would win a husband; but in France they would run round the fires nine times to obtain the same outcome.

Ashes to Ashes The by-product of the fires had their own magical efficacy. The ashes, placed in hen's nests, would encourage the laying of eggs. If they were mixed with cattle's drinking water, the herd would thrive.

Solstice festival In Belarus, the solstice festival, the most popular in the calendar, is known as Kupalle. Nowadays this name is said to be taken from a Christian saint called Ivan Kupala, although in pre-Christian times the name was traced to a lunar goddess, Kupala.

Wreaths There are various types of fortune-telling on Kupalle night. Girls can float wreaths of flowers on the river, and the ones whose wreaths get entangled with other plants can look forward to early marriage. If a plantain leaf is picked at a crossroads and placed under a pillow, it will bring dreams of a future spouse. If a couple can see the flower of a fern magically glowing, as it does on Kupalle night, they will live happily and, better still, would have the gift of foreseeing the future. On that night, too, trees can talk and walk from place to place.

Kupalle fires The fires that are lit on Kupalle night have magical powers. If you burn flax plants in the fires and sing a special chant, you can make the crops flourish. Coals from the fire can be scattered among crops to promote their health. And, as in other countries, cattle are driven through the fire to purify them. Children can be brought close to the fire to bring them spiritual well-being, and the clothes of the sick can be dried on the fire to bring health.

THE SATURNALIA

Every year, on December 17, Ancient Rome would give itself over to seven days of orgy called the Saturnalia. The festival was named after the god Saturn, who had once been a king of Italy and had taught the people the arts of agriculture as he presided over a golden age of peace, equality, and virtue. During the Saturnalia the Romans decked their homes with evergreens and exchanged gifts. In each group of revelers a King of the Festival would be selected, who would play all manner of jokes, issue ludicrous commands, and see to it that the merriment was sustained.

In the less civilized past, this figure would have ended his rule by being ritually sacrificed on the altar of Saturn, and this practice long continued in the outposts of the Roman Empire. The early Christian martyr St. Dasius was a Roman soldier garrisoned on the river Danube who in A.D. 303 was elected King of the Feast. Even though he knew he was soon to die, as a Christian he refused to act with the necessary licentiousness, and was beheaded.

The most amazing feature of the Saturnalia was the total reversal of the roles of menials and their social superiors. In each home, the servants could say whatever they wished and behave as they wished, completely safe from punishment. At meals they could eat and drink as they liked and their masters would even wait on them at table.

Hinduism

MAKING BOYS INTO MEN

A boy of the Brahmin caste makes the transition into *brahmacharya,* the "disciplined living" of adulthood, in an elaborate ritual. Traditionally, he is sent to a special residential school, which may be a monastery. One of the names for this separation from home is "half-marriage." Before his departure he must learn certain Hindu rituals, must overcome his attachment to his mother, and must learn symbolic begging. His sisters bathe him. The older women teach him basic household arts that he will need to look after himself at school: such as drawing water from the well, and preparing food. His head is shaved all over and he bathes again, is decorated with ritual dyes and garlands, and goes through a ceremony to bring him into bachelorhood. He then begs symbolically from the guests, who respond with gifts.

INSTANT DUNG

One of the Hindu purification rituals requires the use of cow dung. Modern Hindus, especially those living in cities, are increasingly neglecting this aspect of their religious obligations because they object to the foul smell. An enterprising company in Calcutta (Kolkata) is now selling instant dung. The user just needs to add water to give the dung the needed consistency. Camphor, turmeric and sandalwood are included in the material to make the dung less offensive.

DIWALI

The festival of Diwali is also called the Festival of Lights. It falls on variable dates during July or August. It occurs at the end of the monsoon season, when the heavy seasonal rains have ended The monsoons bring insects and the threat of rot and mold in homes, so houses must be meticulously cleaned, perhaps repainted, and then decorated to make them bright and welcoming. Only if the house is attractive will Lakshmi, the goddess of good luck and wealth, wish to visit. If she does not, it will be visited instead by her brother, bringer of bad things. During the five-day festival, now observed by many non-Hindus, everyone wears their best clothes, friends and neighbors visit each other and sumptuous meals are eaten. There are firework displays at night, and candles are floated on the rivers in little boats.

Buddhist Kalachakra Initiation

THE WHEEL OF TIME

As part of their progress toward enlightenment, Buddhist monks participate in a great ritual called the Kalachakra Initiation. Kalachakra is a deity whose name means "Wheel of Time," which is the great cycle of birth and rebirth that Buddhists believe all living things go through on their way toward enlightenment. The core of the ritual is the construction, contemplation, and destruction of a great circular picture called a mandala, representing the Wheel.

The ritual begins with the assembling of the monks in a special building called the *thekpu*. Everything in the *thekpu* is of the finest workmanship. The ritual is presided over by the Vajra Master, or ritual master. It begins with the monks' representative requesting that the Master begin the ceremony. The Master then calls on the spirits of the place to assent to the proceedings. The reluctance of the spirits has to be overcome by the monks' Earth Dance. When the assent of the Earth Spirit, on behalf of all the local spirits, has been obtained, the construction of the mandala begins. All the materials used in it must be blessed in the numerous rituals of the following days.

Over the next two days the Vajra Master creates construction lines by snapping a stretched string, soaked in liquid chalk, against the floor. The next day he rubs out parts of the lines to make entrance-ways for the hundreds of deities, including Kalachakra himself, who will occupy the mandala. He puts down grains of wheat to be their cushions. Then the monks pour colored sand to build up the design. After eight days the image is completed, and it is curtained off so that it cannot be seen until the proper time, and there is music and dancing in celebration. The student monks come to the *thekpu* for initiation. They receive the seven Childhood Initiations, each corresponding to a significant event in the life of a child: receiving a name, first bath, first haircut, ears being pierced, saying the first word and so on. At last the new monks can view the Kalachakra mandala. Seven feet across, it represents both the palace in which the gods and goddesses live and the types and levels of enlightenment. It has four quarters, corresponding to the four directions of the compass. It contains symbols, pictures, and Sanskrit word roots. Among its thousands of elements are 722 deities, animals, plants and jewels. At the center is the eight-petaled lotus, representing the bliss of enlightenment, in which resides Kalachakra embracing his female counterpart, Vishvamata.

The final rites are conducted, and the deities depart. Then the mandala is destroyed, the action symbolizing the Buddhist view of the impermanence of all things. The Vajra Master cuts through the mandala with a ritual implement, the monks gather up the sand and it is ceremonially placed into some nearby body of water, mixing the peace of Kalachakra with the world. The ritual and the mandala have traditionally been kept strictly secret from those other than Buddhist monks. But in recent years the Dalai Lama, wishing to improve the world's understanding of Tibetan Buddhism, has presided over the ceremony and let others view the mandala, before it is destroyed in the customary way.

Indigenous Peoples

PENTECOST ISLANDERS

The youths of Pentecost Island, one of the Vanuatu group in the South Pacific, invented the prototype of bungee jumping centuries ago. It makes the modern Western form of the sport look wimpy. Bungee jumpers use reliable elastic cables and know precisely how far they will fall according to their weight and the height they are jumping from. They jump over water or a soft surface. By contrast, the divers of Pentecost Island leap above land—admittedly, soft ground—that has been dug over immediately before the ritual begins. The jumper's fall is sharply broken by almost non-elastic vines tied around his ankles. Only the experienced judgment of a tribal elder assures him that the vine will hold and not snap.

The Pentecost Island land-divers perform their ritual around harvest-time, which is usually in May. They believe that the higher the jumps they make, the better their crops will grow. They jump from platforms on a wooden tower that they have themselves constructed. The tower is up to 100 feet high, and is built around a tall tree on a hillside. Each diver builds his own platform that is designed to break when it is jerked by the fall of the diver, which cushions the shock. The jumper's head should stop just above the ground, but often the jumpers hit the ground, more or less gently, and sometimes they suffer broken bones. Only one jumper has died in living memory.

Like all good rituals, land-diving has its legendary origin. Although the practice is now confined to men and boys, it is supposed to have begun with a woman. Fleeing her angry husband, she climbed a high tree, but he followed. Then she leaped, but he jumped after her. Unknown to him, she had been wise enough to tie lianas around her ankles, and she lived while he died.

STAGES IN THE MASAI LIFE

The Masai (or Maasai), the tall, slender warriors and cattle-herders of East Africa, pass through an extraordinary sequence of rites of passage throughout their lives. These mark the transitions from infancy to manhood, becoming a fully fledged warrior, a senior warrior, and finally leaving the ranks of the warriors to pass through the stages of becoming an elder. The Masai make this progress through life in the company of their "age-set;" those who are close to them in age. A new age-set is formed every ten years. For each ritual a ceremonial village of 30 to 40 huts is built. These are just a few highlights of the rituals:

Before boys can be circumcised, they must go through a pre-circumcision ceremony. One boy is chosen to be the chief of his age-set. This is a misfortune for him, because he is regarded as having taken on his peers' sins. The ceremony itself involves day-long dancing.

When the boys reach puberty, it is time for circumcision. For seven days beforehand the boys herd cattle. On their way to the ceremony they are at turns encouraged and taunted by men and other boys: in mocking songs they are told that if they run away or struggle against the knife, they will be killed or cast out of the tribe. No pain-killers are used in the operation and the effects take months to heal. After the ceremony, the boys receive gifts of cattle, and having become men, are permitted to carry a warrior's spear, to tend large herds, to travel alone at night.

Later in life, having graduated to the status of a senior warrior, he goes through the meat ceremony. A bull is slaughtered and consumed. Then it is necessary for wives to prove to their husbands that they have not been unfaithful with men from a younger age-set. (It is perfectly all right for a wife to have lovers among men of the same age-set.) The warriors establish this by wrestling matches among themselves. How close they can come to the hide of the slaughtered bull determines how fortunate they have been. When a wife is judged to have been unfaithful, she must buy her way back into her husband's favor with a cow given by her family.

The Masai man becomes a full elder in a special ceremony. On the morning of that day, he is given a special elder's chair, in which he sits while he is shaved by his eldest wife. The chair will stay with him as a lucky possession until it breaks. If it is unbroken at the time of his death, his eldest son will claim possession of it.

CANNIBALISM

Cannibalism is an honored tradition in many cultures. It was even known among the Ancient Greeks. According to the historian Herodotus, the Calations, considered it a duty to consume their revered kinsfolk when they died.

Ashes A variant was practiced by one Queen Artemisia, who mixed the ashes of a dead lover with wine, and drank it.

Australian aboriginals used to eat slain enemies, and also their dead kinsfolk. There were very strict rules specifying which relatives were permitted to eat someone. In the Mara tribe, for example, there were four groupings, called the Mumbali, the Kuial, the Murungun, and the Purdal. The rules about eating the dead were:

a Mumbali was eaten by Kuial and Murungun;

a Kuial was eaten by Mumbali and Purdal;

a Murungun was eaten by Mumbali and Purdal;

a Purdal was eaten by Kuial and Murungun.

When someone died, a man would wrap the body in bark and leave it till the morning. Male cousins—specifically, sons of the dead person's maternal uncles—did the cooking. They would light a fire in a pit far from the main camp and heat stones in it. The dead person's hair would be cut off and burned. Bark would be laid over the hot stones, the body placed on that and another layer of bark put over the corpse. Then the hole would be filled in. When the body was sufficiently cooked, it was removed from the ground, laid on bark, and cut up.

Men, women and children in the permitted groups were allowed to take part in the feast, and enjoyed it. Then the bones of the deceased were wrapped in bark and placed on a tree platform. The camp had to move immediately to a new location, because the frightening spirit of the dead person would haunt the old location to see that all the ceremonies were properly carried out. Only when they were completed would it be free to leave to return to its original home.

After some months men of the correct grouping would take the bones, now clean after exposure to the weather, from the platform. They would pull the bones apart, smash the skull into fragments, and then bury them all, except the long arm-bones. The tree would be burned, and the arm-bones would be wrapped in bark and handed to the mother. She would cradle them and wail all day and night.

It might be several years later that the bones were taken back from the mother, placed in a decorated log coffin. After many complex rituals, the coffin was finally placed among rocks on a hillside, or placed in the branches of a tree, and was left for nature to take its course.

Cannibals disgusted by cannibalism One of the last peoples to be forced to give up cannibalism is the Wari' tribe of Amazonia. The outside world had no dealings with them prior to the 1950s. Until recently it was their practice to eat the bodies of their deceased relatives and enemies whom they had vanquished.

Eating your own Eating dead enemies was a way of triumphing over them, and perhaps fits the idea of cannibalism that has long prevailed in the West. Cannibalism of dead kin was a way of healing the grief of the survivors, and giving the dead a decent exit from the world. Reminders of the dead were erased: their house was burned, their name was not spoken. After three days in the steaming Amazonian heat, decomposition would be well under way. The body would be cut up, and parts would be cooked and eaten. It would not be the closest relatives, but the in-laws who would eat the flesh. Remarkably, they found the process revolting, because the Wari' loathe putrefaction. They forced themselves to complete the act as a pious duty. In a symbolic sense, however, the whole tribe would get the chance to eat the deceased. The Wari' believe that the dead return as peccaries—wild pigs— that the tribe lives on. Thus the dead continue to offer sustenance to the living. Nowadays the Wari', whose numbers are down to 2,000, bury their dead as the authorities compel them to do. They say they find it hard to accept the thought of their loved ones' bodies decaying in cold, wet soil.

Cannibal attack Black magic involving murder and an element of cannibalism survives in some areas of the world today. One such place is Guyana. The magic, and the person who practices it, are both called *kanaimà*. The sorcerer will physically attack a victim, inflicting injuries that will linger for months or years. Then he will follow up with an attack with weapons and poisons that inflict fatal damage, though the death is designed to be as lingering and agonizing as possible. Three days after the death, the *kanaimà* will poke a stick into the putrefying corpse, extract some of the ooze from it, and lick it. This touch of cannibalism is necessary to protect the sorcerer against vengeance from the dead person's kin. The crime appears not to be directed against the victim personally, but to be a ritual designed to propitiate the gods and keep the world running smoothly.

New Guinea The peoples of New Guinea, in the South Pacific, practiced cannibalism of their defeated enemies. They would do this in the magnificently decorated structures called spirit houses. The spirit houses were the places where
initiated men gathered for religious rituals, prepared to set out in hunting parties and on war raids, and where the spirits of the ancestors visited the tribe.
The roofs were supported with elaborately carved pillars, war shields lined the
walls, and the heads of victims who had been eaten would be mounted over the
entrances to warn away women and uninitiated men.

Body count Jean de Léry, a sixteenth-century missionary, recorded that the
natives of Brazil were honored by their peers for their acts of cannibalism.
After a cannibal feast, they would return to their homes, make cuts in their
arms, chests and thighs, and rub black powder into them to make them into
permanent scars. The highest respect went to men with the greatest number
of scars on their bodies.

Scar Face Another missionary recorded slightly different customs in another tribe.
Here the scarring preceded the cannibalism. And the business of making the scars
and recovering was a full-blown ritual, with the man spending days not moving
from his bed while the scars healed.

HUMAN SACRIFICE

Fiji is associated with a dark past of human sacrifice. The lives of the people were
tightly enclosed by superstition and magical belief, and many of the most important events in community life, such as the installation of a chief, could only take

place over a pile of human bodies. When a temple or chief's house was built, victims were buried alive to "hold up" the building, as they described it. When war canoes were launched, it was over the bodies of living victims, giving the craft a baptism of blood. The victims were cooked and eaten afterward. The power of the Fijian chiefs was absolute, and a strict protocol governed the behavior of their subjects in their presence. The commoners had to get out of the chief's path, put down any objects they were carrying, kneel, clap their hands, and call out certain words of respect. They could not enter the chief's house by the door that was reserved for him alone. Any infringement of these rules would result in their joining the ritual of human sacrifice—as a victim.

RITES OF PASSAGE

Native Americans The native peoples of North America often included terrifying ordeals among their rites, especially those marking the stages along the way of manhood. A major ceremony among many tribes was the Sun Dance, a summer ritual lasting several days. There would be fasting, sacrifices, prayers, dancing, and singing. With some tribes, wooden skewers would pierce the participants' chests, and thongs would connect the skewers to a central pole, around which the men would dance until the skewers broke free of the flesh. The pain and the exhaustion involved in this ceremony could induce ecstatic visions in the participants.

Among American Indian tribes boys entered into flourishing manhood only when they had been visited by a vision from the spirit world. The vision would be in the form of an animal or bird and for the rest of his life would become that person's personal totem: that is, would be in a special relationship to him, a sort of mystical brotherhood. Though the vision might come in a dream without any effort on the boy's part, it was usual to have to seek it through a "vision quest." This began at about the age of eleven. The boy would fast for days, pray to the sun, and go through punishing ordeals, such as cutting off one joint of a finger. The totem he acquired would determine his life path: he might become a warrior, or perhaps a healer or shaman (priest-magician). The boy who failed to see a vision was destined for an ignominious and impoverished life.

Nigeria The Ohafia people of southeastern Nigeria recognize one stage in a boy's transition to manhood around the age of seven. The boy is given his first bow and arrows then, and he is expected in due course to kill a small bird with them. When he does so, he parades through his village in ceremonial clothes with the bird tied to the end of the bow, singing triumphant songs, which include plenty of derision aimed at his age-mates who have not yet equaled his feat. Sometimes the boy has killed his bird with a modern-style slingshot from the market, which is more powerful and accurate than the traditional bow—but if so, he keeps the fact secret.

Aborigines Among the aborigines of Australia, it was the custom to send each boy away for secret ceremonies of initiation into manhood. While he was away, those remaining would hear loud, terrifying roaring noises coming across the miles of desert. The women and girls were taught that this was the voice of a great spirit that carried the boys off during initiation. The boy, meanwhile, learned a secret of initiation: that the noise was made by a bull-rarer, a piece of stone with a hole in it, tied to string, which was twirled round a man's head to create the noise. The boy was sworn to secrecy and supposedly the women were never any the wiser.

Italy A boy on the eve of puberty is traditionally put through a ritual intended to bless his later life. He is passed between the two halves of a split sapling, three times. Inside the sapling is a small picture of the Virgin Mary. The halves of the sapling are tied together, with the picture inside, so the Virgin will watch over him.

Modern Cults

BLOOD RITUAL

The Aum Shinrikyo cult, which began in Japan in the 1980s, worshipped its founder, Shoko Asahara, as a god. Since his birth this man had been blind in one eye and only partially sighted in the other. He was a timid child, but overcame his disabilities with ferocious extravagance. The worship by his followers strengthened him to the point where he encouraged his cult to mount a nerve-gas attack on the Tokyo subway in March 1995: 5500 people were affected, and 12 of them died. On the road to this crime, Asahara had stoked the devotion of his followers with ever more extravagant practices. Asahara's followers made tea by boiling his beard clippings in water. Asahara ended by inviting his followers to join in a commercial, near-cannibal ritual: to sit together in a room and ceremonially drink his blood from small glasses, sold to them at $7,000 per dose.

SPIRITUAL PUSH

The Aetherius Society is a flying-saucer religion that, according to its literature, has time and again saved the world from the machinations of enemies in outer space and the misguided actions of the human race. The society was founded in the 1950s by George King, an Englishman who in May 1954 was told by a disembodied voice, "Prepare yourself! You are to become the voice of Interplanetary Parliament." Among the purposes of the society are to spread the teachings of the Cosmic Masters. These include Jesus, who was a Venusian, and Aetherius, from the same planet. A picture of Jesus and another of George King (who died in 1997), preside over the weekly meetings of the society. Among the prayers, taped messages, recorded by King and by various interplanetary messengers, are played.

These rituals are ordinary enough. More extraordinary ones are occasionally played out. The Aetherius Society believes the well-being of the world depends on spiritual energy stored in 19 mountains around the world. Nine are in Britain, four in the United States, and the rest are in Europe, Africa, and Australia. From 1959 to 1961, in "Operation Starlight," King and his close companions went on several expeditions up these mountains in order to place "spiritual batteries" on their peaks. As with any pilgrimage, it wasn't all plain sailing: when climbing Castle Peak in Colorado, which is over 14,000 feet, they came close to death because of the harsh weather conditions encountered.

The peaks release their spiritual energies when pilgrims climb them and pray with unselfish motives. Aetherius Society members continue to make regular journeys to these holy mountains to engage in rituals to tap into and release their energies.

The spiritual batteries, recharged by the prayers of the society's members, help to keep the world safe from war and environmental catastrophe, both natural and manmade. But from time to time an extra spiritual push (as it is called) is needed. Prayer activity is redoubled, while a giant spaceship called Satellite 3, moves in close to the earth, and pumps spiritual energy down to us. The need will remain for a long time to come: Master Aetherius has explained that Satellite 3 will be doing its work for many centuries.

Earth dwellers have good friends on Mars. The Martians intervened during the last century, at great cost to themselves, to protect us from intelligent fish dwelling on the planet Garouche, on the other side of the Galaxy, who tried to remove earth's atmosphere. George King himself was nearly killed three times during the battle. The prayers of his followers in the Aetherius Society continue to keep earth in contact with our interplanetary friends

THE CULTS OF CARGO

Since the late nineteenth century over a broad swathe of the South Pacific, at least 70 different local religions have been created that anthropologists call "cargo cults." Their doctrines vary, but all basically believe that soon a new age of prosperity will commence for their adherents. This age will arrive when the ships, and latterly the planes, that hitherto have brought food and luxuries to the white people, will begin to bring them to the native peoples of the area.

Often they teach that white people have intercepted goods that always were intended for the aboriginal people. To be prepared for that day, the cargo cultists build imitation jetties for ships, clear landing strips for planes, build life-size models of planes to go on them, and erect wooden facsimiles of control towers. They conduct ceremonies to welcome the goods that are always, year after year, about to appear. They don mock headphones and talk into mock microphones, and signal to the sky. It makes perfectly good sense to them: if similar rituals bring goods to the whites, why should they not be equally effective for the native peoples? In the end, they have been vindicated: the cargo cultists are now on the tourist routes, and their rituals now bring in tourist cash.

BURNING MAN

The need for ritual is so deeply ingrained that in today's world it seems that rituals can be invented without needing to be attached to any particular system of belief. A ritual that was established in 1986 and is still going from strength to strength takes place every year in the Nevada Desert, around the beginning of September. It has grown from its beginnings on a San Francisco beach until it now includes over 25,000 people, who converge on a playa, or flat lake-bed, in the Black Rock Desert. Many of them are devotees of magic, earth worship, Satanism, and assorted New Age beliefs, but the festival's appeal goes wider than that. All that unites the activities at each festival is a theme devised by the Festival's founder, Larry Harvey, such as Hell or The Body. As in traditional rituals, there are no spectators, only participants. People set up "theme camps," with titles such as Lost Vegas or Motel 666. They bring their own food and drink, and share it. They ride over the desert in and on "mutant vehicles" of their own designs, and live in shelters they have built. The week of celebration ends with the burning of a human effigy 40 feet tall. The Burning Man festival has echoes of ancient rituals in which effigies made of straw or wicker were burned—sometimes with sacrificial victims, human or animal, inside them. Such ceremonies have been attributed to the Druids. Versions are kept alive in northern Europe, including Britain, Belgium, France, Germany and Austria.

Straw Man In Aachen, Germany, and in northern France, the ritual takes a slightly different form. A man clad in straw acts the part of the victim. After pulling various pranks and after being chased, he seems to end up on the bonfire. In fact the man inside the costume has contrived to slip away.

Green Man In a more sinister Austrian ritual, a boy clad in green has to go from house to house, collecting wood for the fire in which, notionally, he will be consumed.

Russia In Russia the figure involved in fire ceremonies was a dummy made of straw and was dressed in women's clothes. A tree is felled nearby and is decked with ribbons. In this case, however, a separate fire is lit, and the young people jump this, carrying the straw woman with them. On the day following the celebration the straw figure is cast into a nearby stream.

Other non-Christian Religious Rituals

Tibet Every New Year the Buddhist monks of Tibet demonstrate their prowess in creating sculptures illustrating different stories from their voluminous scriptures. They can be up to 30 feet high. They are an apt embodiment of the Buddhist view that all things are impermanent, because the scriptures are made of butter.

Taoist In late September and early October in Thailand, a nine-day Taoist festival begins to introduce a period of fasting. After five days of street processions and religious ceremonials, feats of endurance begin. On day six, devotees run over red-hot charcoal. On day seven, they run barefoot up and down tall ladders, whose rungs have been replaced with sharp blades.

Then there are two days with further processions through the town, but this time the frenzied worshippers do their utmost to mortify their own and each other's flesh. They stick iron skewers, meters long, into each other's bodies; they hoist each other off the ground by steel hooks piercing their bare flesh.

It is claimed that participants come through these ordeals unscathed. Tradition has it that these rituals began 150 years ago when members of a traveling Chinese opera company that was visiting the country fell ill. Mutual acts of mortification appeased the gods and restored them to health.

Rituals from Around the World

BRITAIN

Twelfth Night Englishmen used to go out into the orchards on Twelfth Night, carrying their weapons and well fortified with drink. They would form a circle around the oldest tree, chant a traditional song, and fire their guns (loaded only with powder not shot) at the tree. They wouldn't be allowed inside until they had guessed what meal was being prepared by the womenfolk. The man who guessed correctly was named King for the Evening, and presided over the merrymaking.

Hobby horse Bucolic rituals are kept alive in English villages and towns today. In the coastal town of Minehead, in Somerset, Mayday is celebrated with the help of a hobbyhorse, which is a construction worn by a man and very little resembling a horse, but possessing a rudimentary "mouth" and a rope "tail." This particular hobbyhorse is pretty rowdy, and a great drinker. It starts its activities on the night before Mayday, making its way from pub to pub, accompanied by a raucous group of musicians. It is likely to butt or lash with its tail any passerby who doesn't make a contribution to charity on the spot.

The hobbyhorse continues similar activities throughout the week, during which it does battle with the Town Horse, another of its kind. May 3, is Bootie Night, when any passerby may be caught by the horse's attendants and gently butted ("booted") ten times, and then made to dance a jig with the horse.

At Padstow, not very far away in Cornwall, they also have a licentious hobbyhorse, known locally as the 'obby 'oss, which indulges in very similar antics. It also likes to grab women that it meets and rub soot on their faces; they are assured that this will bring them good luck and fertility.

Dressing the wells Derbyshire is probably the part of England where the custom of annual well-dressing is maintained most vigorously. The wells are adorned with ribbons, garlands and floral compositions on Biblical themes. The celebrations originate in rituals of thanksgiving to God from the days when all village life depended on the waters vouchsafed by the wells. Sometimes the thanks were being offered for the well sustaining the people when their neighbors were suffering drought; or for keeping a village healthy when the land was ravaged by the plague. In some villages, well-dressing has been brought up to date in the custom of dressing the faucets of the home.

Beating the bounds Many English parishes still observe the custom, universal in the days before reliable printed maps became widely available, of "beating the bounds." Clergy, local notables, and local children would walk in procession around the boundary of the parish. The children were "beaten" (though only symbolically) with willow wands, to impress on them the parish limits. They would even take dips in streams and ponds on the way.

Burning Barrels In the seventeenth century the town of Ottery St. Mary in Devon seems to have felt a need to cleanse its streets of evil. In doing so it began its Festival of Burning Barrels. The barrels are soaked for weeks beforehand in tar. Each is lit outside the local pub that sponsors it, and soon burns fiercely. Then it's lifted onto someone's shoulders and carried around the town, whose streets are crowded with onlookers. Some are carried by women or children; at the end of the evening, heavier ones, weighing well over 60 pounds, are being carried by men. It is a matter of great pride to take part, and generations of the same families carry some of the barrels. All this happens on Bonfire Night, November 5, when effigies of Guy Fawkes, who plotted to blow up the king and Parliament in 1605, are being burned all over the country.

The Randwick Wap The small Gloucestershire village of Randwick has a peculiar custom called the Wap, which is performed early in May. The word "wap" comes from the old "wappenshaw," meaning "weapon showing," but no weapons are in evidence nowadays. A special part of the event is called the "fracas," in which villagers in fancy costumes of the Tudor and Regency periods make a procession from the village war memorial to the Mayor's Pool. Leading the way is the Mop Man, carrying a wet mop which he applies to as many bystanders as come within reach. The mayor and the Festival Queen are carried shoulder-high until they reach the pool, into which the mayor is dunked.

Cheese-rolling Randwick (see the Randwick Wap, described above) also indulges its eccentricity by engaging in cheese-rolling. The Sunday before the Wap, three large cheeses are rolled anticlockwise around Randwick Church. This is said to ward off evil spirits. One is cut up and distributed to the crowds. But the Randwick obsession with cheese goes further than this. Following the Wap, everyone assembles on a local hill and watches contestants chase a 25-pound cheese as it rolls down the very steep hillside. The same madness is enacted around the same date at nearby Cooper's Hill. The two events between them rack up dozens of serious injuries, keeping the local hospitals busy.

Woolsack Races The British obsession with running up and down steep hills is in full evidence at Gumstool Hill, Tetbury, in Gloucestershire, at the end of May. That's when teams of four race up and down the one-in-four gradient, carrying woolsacks weighing 60 pounds (for the men's teams) or 35 pounds (for the ladies' teams). Thee are events for solo participants as well. The event is 300 years old and was apparently started as a test of prowess by young cattle drovers.

St. Briavels Bread and Cheese Dole The village of St. Briavels in Gloucestershire displays a sudden loss of decorum on Whit Sunday each year, the Bread and Cheese Dole takes place. Pieces of bread and cheese are thrown from baskets to crowds waiting to catch them. Recipients dressed in medieval costume are fiercely keen to get the greatest possible share of the offerings. Their costumes are often craftily adapted to this end: wide skirts and broad-brimmed hats are very useful for gathering large quantities of flying food. The ritual dates from the twelfth century, when grabbing a share of the food was a deadly serious business—not least because it was also regarded as bringing good luck. Some of the morsels were kept as charms rather than eaten. The drunkenness and fighting that once went with the ritual seem now to belong in the past.

State Opening of Parliament The proceedings of the United Kingdom Parliament are thick with rituals, some of which date back to the fourteenth century. Like all rituals, they are designed to keep ancient memories alive, even if in a dim and confused form, in order to protect a valuable tradition. At the time of the annual State Opening of Parliament, the official opening of the parliamentary session for the year, many rituals are in evidence that are connected with the constitutional relationship between the Crown, the House of Lords and the House of Commons. The opening is presided over by the monarch, in crown and regalia, though her authority is now purely symbolic. The opening takes place in the chamber of the House of Lords, once the senior of the two houses of parliament. It has long since reduced to the status of a revising chamber that, in a conflict with the Commons, can at most delay legislation. The elected members of Parliament are summoned from the House of Commons to attend on Her

Majesty. An official called Black Rod—or in full, the Gentleman Usher of the Black Rod—is dispatched from the House of Lords to summon the MPs. As he approaches the doors of the Commons, they are slammed in his face, as a reminder of the independence of the elected house. He raps three times on the doors with the ebony cane that gives him his title. Once admitted, he informs the MPs that the monarch awaits them, and then he leads them in procession to the Lords. The peers of the realm (lords and ladies) are already seated, and there is room only for a representative group of MPs to stand in the chamber while they hear the "Most Gracious Speech from the Throne," a statement of the government's program for the coming year, read by the monarch.

Similar versions of the same rituals are enacted in parliaments of countries that were once part of the British Empire. In Canada, Black Rod summons the members of the House of Commons to the Senate chamber to hear the Speech from the Throne, which again is the government's legislative program, read by the Governor-General. In the single-chamber parliaments of the Canadian provinces and territories, a black rod is used by the Sergeant-at-Arms to knock on doors and gain admittance for the Lieutenant-Governor, so he can read the Speech from the throne.

GREECE

Role reversal for a day The Festival of Women is held on January 8, every year in the towns of Monoklissia and Nea Petra. For this one day, it's the women who are looked after by the men. The men stay at home cooking, cleaning and looking after the children. The women meanwhile head off to the cafes, where they drink coffee and ouzo and play backgammon. In the evening, the women enjoy meals prepared by the men in the local *tavernas* (bar-restaurants).

INDIA

Camel Festival The importance of camels in the life of Rajasthan, in northwest India, is reflected in the camel festival held every January in the ancient walled town of Bikaner, with its sixteenth-century fort. The major events include camel races, of course, but also "beauty competitions," in which the merits of especially fine beasts are assessed, as in any horse or cattle show. The proceedings begin with a parade in which the cherished animals are put into clown dress.

IRAN

Praying for rain In Iran, peoples remote from the urban centers still offer rituals, prayers to bring rain when drought strikes. A scarecrow can be jigged around in a dance during the ceremony. And, most bizarre of all, a selected person may be pushed into water to make sure that divine powers get the hint. The lucky victim may be a middle-aged woman, a *Seyed* (descendant of the Prophet Mohammed), or an identical twin—or, better still, both the twins.

Down the drain In yet another ritual, women will mix flour and water, climb onto the roof of a mosque, and pour the mixture down the drainpipe, greeting its arrival at the ground with yells and songs.

Mass prayers will be said in the desert. The women and children pray in groups separated from the men, so that God can clearly hear their cries. Then the participants march in a procession, and villagers on a rooftop sacrifice a precious bucket of water by pouring it over them, as if they were getting the benefit of a downpour. A donkey skull in which a seed has taken root will improve the efficacy of the ritual.. Children may paint the skull red and mount it on a stick while singing songs invoking rain. Then they burn it in a bonfire before throwing it into a well and throwing stones at it until it breaks. Surprisingly, the donkey's skull is linked to a figure that is viewed not as evil but as good. This beast is described as a donkey, but it has three legs, nine mouths, six eyes, and a horn. According to myth, it comes to the aid of Tishter, the water goddess, who takes the form of a white horse in her battle against the evil spirit who would deny water to the world.

ITALY

Ivrea Orange Fight Ivrea lies in the very north of Italy. Its lengthy carnival culminates in three days of mayhem: a battle fought with oranges in the streets of the town, while a bonfire blazes in the square. In the public mind it is linked with Napoleon, who invaded and ruled this area in the early 1800s.

Many of the combatants wear fancy dress, predictably there are many Napoleons to be seen on the streets and the populace, on foot, engage hooded enemies on horse-drawn wagons that race around the streets. The last day of fighting is on Shrove Tuesday.

The flower festival of Monterosso Once a year the streets of the Italian town of Monterosso in the Cinqueterre (or Five Lands), of northwestern Italy are elaborately decorated with impermanent artworks: pictures created with flower petals and food items. They can be admired for just a few hours: then a church procession marking the Feast of Corpus Domini marches through the streets— and over the artworks. Still, there's always the next festival to look forward to in Monterosso: not just the Festival of Lemons and the Festival of Times Past but also the Festival dedicated jointly to the Salted Anchovy and Olive Oil.

The Battle of the Bridge The city of Pisa, in Tuscany, has long known rivalry between its different quarters. From time immemorial this has been acted out in the Battle of the Bridge, which now takes place on the last Saturday of June. "Armies' from the city's quarters, arrayed in magnificent armor, and marching under splendid banners, draw up at the a bridge crossing the River Arno. In the center of the bridge is a seven-ton trolley, running on tracks 55 yards long. The battle is between Tramontana, north of the river, and Mezzogiorno, to the south. The aim of the 20-man teams is to push the trolley to the opposite end of the bridge, running over the enemy's standard. There are several bouts in the course of the day.

The modern ritual avoids the bloodshed that was common in earlier days. One story says that the battle was originated by Pelops, the legendary Greek founder of Pisa, who was nostalgic for the Olympic Games of his homeland. Another regards it as a kind of gladiatorial combat decreed by the Roman Emperor Hadrian.

JAPAN

Tofu Shrine An old Buddhist ritual of Japan takes place every December. All the broken and bent pins and needles collected in the household are taken to a special shrine prepared in the corner of a room. There is a pan of tofu (soybean curd) in the shrine. The broken or bent needles are inserted into this one by one, while a prayer of thanks is said over the item for the useful work it has done for the family. Finally the participants wrap the tofu in paper, and float it out to sea, where it soon sinks.

The Naked Man Festival At Kounomiya Shrine in Inazawa City a man is selected for the coveted honor of being the center of attention at the rite. He goes through a ritual of purification in which he is stripped naked and has his body hair shaved off. He then runs through crowds of thousands of Japanese men—as many as 9,000—themselves dressed only in loincloths and sandals. They beat him as he passes. All the bad luck of the men taking part passes from them into the naked man when they succeed in making contact with him, which is why the ritual is so popular. He carries on like this for at least an hour before he is carried to the shrine. Here he takes part in prayer before being allowed to dress again. He is then chased out of town.

Coming-of-Age Day In Japan, January 14 is celebrated as Coming-of-Age Day by all who have turned 20 in the previous year. These young people can now vote and can legally smoke and drink alcohol. They celebrate by going in their smartest clothes to a Shinto shrine, with their friends and family. The young women traditionally wear special white fur collars with their kimonos. There's even more fun afterward, when they go to a large meeting where officials deliver homilies. Then it's off to a celebration dinner.

One week later, the ceremony continues with an archery contest at a temple in Kyoto. This competition has been held for over 400 years, and today has developed into a purely symbolic ritual. Each participant gets to fire two arrows from a huge seven-foot bow. Few—if any—arrows reach the target, 200 feet away.

Baby Sumo Toddlers who have just learned to walk are pitted against each other in a "crying baby sumo" bout in some places in Japan. The children wear elaborate sumo wrestling loincloths and are supported by adults who hold them and gently push them against each other. It's the first baby to cry who is the loser, or in some places, who is the winner. Since in Japan crying is held to encourage healthy growth, the whole procedure is a ritualized way of bringing prosperity to the children; all of whom go home with a prize.

Firewalking at Mount Takao Mount Takao near Tokyo is the home of the Hiwatari firewalking festival, held in March every year. In the 1950s it was made open to all—even to foreign visitors. The Buddhist priests of the Shingon sect have for centuries hardened themselves here in ascetic rituals. At the firewalking festival, a huge bonfire is built and the *yamabushi,* or mountain-dwelling priests, conduct rituals to drive away evil spirits and expel the sins of the participants. Pieces of wood that have been rubbed against sick parts of the body and on which the sufferers' names have been written are thrown into the fire. When the flames have subsided, the *yamabushi* walk on the intensely hot cinders, followed by the other participants. The ritual will protect them, they believe, from misfortune through the year to come. So will the cinders which often taken home as a good-luck charm.

KOREA

Preparation for birth In Korea, as is the case in many Asian countries, male children are deeply desired, female ones less so. Rituals have existed since time immemorial to ensure that a new child is a boy. Superstitious women still pray and make offerings over periods of weeks or even months to a host of divinities, including sacred trees and rocks, and even to the stars that make up the Big Dipper constellation. When the pregnancy is under way, the success of these attempts can be divined from various signs. If the mother dreams of fierce animals, it will be a boy. If she dreams of gentle things, such as flowers, it will be a girl.

The grandmother spirit is an important personage to be placated if the birth is to be an easy one and the mother's health assured. And if the future is to be bright for the child, the mother must observe many taboos during the pregnancy. She must not step over a straw rope, approach unclean things, or do anything that is morally wrong. If she eats an excess of duck, the child will waddle like a duck; if she eats too much chicken, the child will have skin like that of a chicken. Numerous other foods must be avoided for similar reasons.

After Birth When the child is born, a straw rope across the gate protects the house from evil spirits and ill-intentioned persons. The afterbirth (placenta) is burned: in the house if more children are desired; or a distance away if they are not. Delicate foods are offered to the grandmother spirit for seven days after the birth.

Enormous care is taken to protect the child's future well-being. People in mourning or who have taken part in a funeral recently are not permitted to enter the house.

In order not to offend the spirits after the birth, or make them jealous of the child, no one praises the child. On the contrary; they gave it humiliating nicknames.

Fortune telling The Korean baby is called on to foretell its own future at the age of one. A party is held, and the baby is placed before a low table on which are all manner of gifts from friends. The baby is encouraged to pick one up. If it picks up a pen or ink bottle, it will be a scholar; cakes portend a government career; a toy weapon, the military; money or rice means that it will be wealthy.

MEXICO

Radish In Mexico on December 23, the country people hold a curious form of sculpture context: their medium is the unusual one of the radish. These vegetables are large but of irregular and twisted form. The whole thing celebrates the arrival of the radish in Mexico on being imported by the Spanish. The craftsmen shape them into scenes from the Bible, legend or history, and cash prizes are awarded.

Joyous Day of the Dead The Day of the Dead is a Mexican festival that has become famous throughout the world. Where most commemorations of the dead in the United States and in most European countries are sad and solemn affairs, the Day of the Dead is an occasion when the spirits of the dead are welcomed back into their old homes and are splendidly entertained.

November 1 is the first day of the festival and is called the Day of the Little Angels, because it is dedicated to children with illnesses. November 2 is dedicated to the adults. Special altars are prepared in private homes, in some part of the house diverted from its normal use. A display is created of mementoes of the loved ones, including some of their cherished possessions, photographs of them—such as a man's pipe, a woman's jewelry, or a child's toys. A path of rose petals may mark the spirits' way from the street door to the altar. A feast is held, at which there is a place for the spirit, with a bowl of water and a cloth to wash his or her hands, and perhaps tobacco if they were a smoker.

Toys, ornaments, and foodstuffs are made in the form of light-hearted representations of skulls, skeletons, and coffins. Among the favorite toys are tissue-paper cutouts called *papel picado*. Sugar skulls decorate the altars. A toy skeleton will be found by one lucky person who shares in the round loaf baked especially for the occasion and called the bread of the dead. Sometimes the loaves are in the shape of a body. Much of the bread bought during the festival is intended to be part of the offerings to the dead. The figure of La Muerte, or Lady Death, in various garbs, is to be seen grinning everywhere.

The living also visit the homes of the dead with night-time vigils held in churchyards. The graves are tended and repaired, and then as beautifully ornamented as the domestic altars earlier in the day. Children's graves are gaily decorated with brightly colored ribbons and streamers. Through the night, candles glow in the churchyards, and sometimes there is music and singing, provided by mariachis, or street bands.

The origins of the Day of the Dead are in a pre-Columbian festival dedicated to the dead and to children. That was held in summer, but the Christian Church converted it into a ritual to be held on All Hallows Eve. Today the customs of Halloween, infiltrating from the north, are being increasingly mixed in with those of the Day of the Dead.

SPAIN

Tomato Festival There's nothing magical, religious, or occult about the Grand Tomato Battle in the Spanish town of Bunyol. It's simply a custom that grew out of a fight in a restaurant in 1945. That little row developed into a food fight, like a scene from a silent-movie comedy. Everyone enjoyed it so much, it was turned into an institution, and is now celebrated each August.

Over 100 tons of ripe tomatoes are trucked into the town in readiness for the combat. Tens of thousands of people from around the world flood into the tiny town, whose normal population is 9,000.

The event begins spectacularly, with rockets fired over the town, releasing their payloads of tomatoes onto the crowds below. Then everyone starts flinging tomatoes at each other. After a couple of hours water tankers are sent in to hose down everything and everyone. The soaking wet veterans finish the day in the bars and cafes.

San Blas Festival San Blas was a saint who is honored every year on February 1 in the town of Almonicid del Marquesado. The streets of the town are invaded by 100 men dressed up as devils. In accordance with the town's conception of what devils should look like, the actors are dressed in clothes resembling pajamas and bishops' miters, and each has a huge cowbell on his backside. The sounds of these bells echo around the town as the devils dance and skip through the streets, doing their best to discomfort any citizen who strays within reach. They continue to the point of exhaustion, and the last devil on his feet is declared the winner.

THAILAND

Water Festival The traditional Thai Water Festival takes place on the Khao San Road, in a district of the capital, Bangkok. It occurs in April, marking the New Year in the Thai calendar. There is little that is religious about it: participants are mostly young Thais and quite a number of foreign visitors. They start proceedings with their own buckets and water guns, but are soon helped out when the municipal water trucks turn up with their power hoses. The water fight continues through the night and the following day, even being taken into restaurants and bars.

Energetic vegetarians The Thai city of Phuket sees a major Vegetarian Festival every year during the ninth lunar month. It invokes the nine Emperor Gods and thousands of warrior spirits, who invade the bodies of the *ma song*, or devotees, during the month-long festival. During this period, the pious people of Phuket abstain from meat, alcohol, and sex, but these privations seem to give them extra energy. During the religious processions, the streets resound to the deafening noise of firecrackers dangled in clusters from bamboo poles and thrust at passersby, or thrown around with abandon. But the astonishing ritual at the heart of the festival is cheek-piercing, carried out on hundreds of *ma song*, both male and female, after they have been put into a trancelike state. Priests drive a heavy metal spike through their cheeks, and then thread some ornamental object through the holes: a string of beads, a skewer, a bunch of flowers.

USA

Groundhog Day Ever since Bill Murray starred in a movie of the same name in 1993, the most famous weather ritual in America has become much more widely known. The ceremony is carried out on February 2. Punxsutawney Phil, a well-fed groundhog, or woodchuck, named for his home town of Punxsutawney, Pennsylvania, begins the day in his heated burrow on Gobbler's Knob hill. He has been moved there the evening before, having spent the previous year living a pampered life in Punxsutawney Library. At 7:25 a.m. on Groundhog Day he is hauled out to perform his sole official duty: to find out whether he can see his own shadow. If he can—in other words, if the day is sunny—the rest of winter, up to the spring equinox, will have bad weather. If he can't see his shadow—that is, if the day is overcast—the rest of the winter will be fine.

The legend of the woodchuck's meteorological skills is recorded as early as 1841. It was said that the groundhog woke from his hibernation, looked out of his burrow, and went back to continue his sleep if he saw his shadow. The story seems to derive from a number of old pieces of weather lore brought from Europe. Traditionally, Candlemas Day, February 2, had weather that was the opposite of what the rest of spring would hold. An English rhyme was:

"If Candlemas be fair and bright,
Winter has another flight.

> If Candlemas brings clouds and rain,
> Winter will not come again."

And from Scotland:

> "If Candlemas Day is bright and clear,
> There'll be two winters in the year."

The groundhog is not native to Europe—Germans traditionally looked out for the shadow of a badger on Candlemas Day.

The ritual at Punxsutawney is now conducted before tens of thousands of people and massed ranks of microphones and T.V. cameras. Punxsutawney Phil is pulled out from under a fake tree stump. The prediction, and its subsequent success, become a matter of public record. It is reported that Punxsutawney Phil's success rate is a meager 39 per cent.

Phony and Made-up Rituals

THE MIRROR WITCH

Teenagers have been scaring themselves for many years with the idea that a suitable invocation before a mirror will summon a malevolent witch that will injure or kill the person carrying out the ritual. In some versions one must say "Bloody Mary!" thirteen times before a mirror in a candlelit room. In another, you must chant the phrase louder and louder while turning around before the mirror, faster and faster. There can be other names for the witch: Hell Mary, Mary Worth, Black Agnes... The ritual is certainly a test of courage: the reckless experimenters half-believe the witch may kill them, or drive them mad, or drag them through the mirror to dwell with her for ever.

DON'T FLASH YOUR LIGHTS!

We like nothing better than to scare ourselves with tales of evil initiation rituals carried out by sinister people for mysterious reasons. Such rituals feature prominently among urban legends—those modern myths spread from person to person, implicitly believed by their purveyors, but always deriving from what "a friend of a friend" told them.

A story that regularly circulates every few years is that prospective new members of tough gangs are required to commit a murder to prove their fitness to join the club. They select their victim in this way: they drive—on bikes if Hell's Angels are the gang in question—at night with their headlights off. The first car to flash its headlights at them in warning marks itself out as the target. The would be gang member follows the victim car and shoots its occupants at the first opportunity.

CASINO AIR

There is a rumor associated with the world of gambling that is completely phony. it is said that casinos pump extra oxygen into their gaming floors during the early hours of the morning, in order to stop tired gamblers going to bed. There is no evidence that this takes place and is an urban myth.

FREEMASONRY

There have always been false stories about the Masons—a highly secretive fraternal society that largely operates through the use of rituals and ceremonies. One of the main rumors about Freemasons is that their rituals are connnected to devil worship and they are said to worship an demonic idol called Baphomet. The Masons strongly deny any connection to Satanism, although rumors still persist.

Another rumor about the Freemasons is that they use their rituals and handshakes in order to recognize each other in everyday life and thereby escaping punishment for immoral or criminal acts. Again, this is disputed by the Masons, who claim that such behavior would have a member expelled.

Superstitions

Bodily Reactions

Even the twitching of an eye is ominous to the superstitious. A twitching of the left eye foretells a death in the family: of the right eye, more happily, a birth.

An eyelash that has fallen out should be put on the back of the hand; then you should make a wish and throw the lash over your shoulder. But if it sticks to your hand, the wish will not be granted.

ITCHING

If occasionally you get that "burning" sensation of heat in your ears, it means that someone is talking about you: and also, according to some, if your right ear itches, someone is speaking well of you; while if the left one itches, someone is speaking badly of you.

If the bottom of your right foot itches, you are going to take a trip.

If the palm of your right hand itches, you will soon be receiving money. But, as usual, left is associated with misfortune: if the palm of your left hand itches, you will soon be paying money out.

If your nose itches, some say, you will soon be kissed by a fool. Others say that an itching nose portends a visitor. Specifically, if it's the right nostril that is itching, the visitor will be female; if it's the left nostril, the visitor will be male.

Touching wood, or knocking on wood, are believed by many to be lucky; but some are less optimistic, and believe only in accordance with an old rhyme:

> "Rub an itch to wood
> It will come to good."

SNEEZING

It used to be believed that sneezing could expel your soul. Saying "God bless you!" protected you.

But in the case of a new-born child, the first sneeze was lucky. Until then the child was under the influence of bad fairies, and until that sneeze came was at risk of becoming a witch or warlock.

A traditional rhyme spells out the significance of sneezing for the superstitious on the different days of the week:

> "Sneeze on a Monday, you sneeze for danger;
> Sneeze on a Tuesday, kiss a stranger;
> Sneeze on a Wednesday, sneeze for a letter;
> Sneeze on a Thursday, something better;

Sneeze on a Friday, sneeze for sorrow;

Sneeze on a Saturday, see your sweetheart tomorrow;

Sneeze on a Sunday, your safety seek;

For Satan will have you the rest of the week."

The omens can become even more complicated when the time of day is taken into account. Some think that it is bad luck to sneeze in the morning before one has one's shoes on. After that, a sneeze before breakfast is lucky, for it means you will have a present. Sneezing on a Saturday night after the lights are lit is unlucky.

Food and Eating

It is thought that biting your tongue while eating betrays the fact that you have told a lie in the recent past.

Before slicing a new loaf of bread, make the sign of the cross on it.

A loaf of bread should never be turned upside down after a slice has been cut from it.

Always eat a fish from the head toward the tail.

Don't get upset if you always burn the onions: a wish made at that moment is bound to come true.

Onions are supposed to have healing powers. Cut one in half and place it under the bed of a sick person, and ignore their protests if they don't like the powerful smell. The strong fragrance is supposed to cure fever and counter harmful toxins in the patient's blood.

We have all heard that spilling salt is unlucky, and that we must throw a pinch over the left shoulder to neutralize the bad luck. The reason, less well known, is that the devil is waiting there, and throwing the salt will disconcert him for a precious moment while the danger passes.

Salt on the doorstep of a new house will help to protect it against evil.

Spilling pepper may not be quite as bad as spilling salt, but it unfortunately does portend a serious argument with your best friend.

A woman should serve her husband roasted owl if she wants him to be obedient to her every wish.

Formerly, in northern England, parties of people would share a dish of carlins, or cooked peas. When the bowl in the middle of the table was almost empty, the diners would take one pea at a time, in turn. The person who took the last pea would be the next to be married.

When shelling peas, you can count yourself lucky if you find a pod containing just one pea, or else nine peas. If you find nine peas in the first pod opened, so much the better. A pod containing nine peas can be rubbed on warts, and then thrown away, while the sufferer chants, "Wart, wart, dry away." This will cure your warts. Alternatively, if a pod with nine peas is too hard to come by, on the day of a new moon touch each wart with a different pea. Then wrap them in a cloth and throw them away backward. This remedy is probably more practically carried out than another traditional one of rubbing one's warts—secretly—against a man who has had an illegitimate child while married.

Pulling the wishbone, or merrythought, of a chicken is a well known way of getting a wish. Two people make a wish silently as they pull at the bone, and whoever gets the bigger piece will have their wish come true; provided they do not tell anyone what the wish was.

There's an extraordinary ritual concerning the wishbone for the person who's desperate to know how long they must wait for marriage. A small hole is drilled in the flat part at the angle of the wishbone. They then balance the wishbone on the bridge of their nose, and try to pass a thread through the hole. The number of unsuccessful tries at this task is the number of years he or she will have to wait before marriage.

Knots

Knots are believed to have magical properties, often malign, in many parts of the world. Tying a knot symbolizes the trapping or binding of a victim; so naturally untying it or cutting it symbolizes the freeing of the person.

In West Africa, knotting a piece of grass would be part of a spell that indicated misfortune or death for someone.

An old German cure for warts consisted of tying knots in a piece of string and leaving it hidden under a stone. Whoever trod on that stone would catch the warts, while the original sufferer would be freed of them.

In many countries it is traditionally bad luck to tie any sort of knot during the marriage service; it can result in a barren marriage. Any knot in the clothing of the bride or groom should be undone during the service.

The pains of childbirth can be eased by undoing all knots in the house, as well as unlocking doors and even unbraiding women's hair.

According to Indian belief, you could be released from fever if a friend could take seven cotton threads to some place where an owl was hooting, and tie a knot at each hoot. Tying the threads around the sufferer's arm was then a certain cure.

A hundred years ago, fishermen in the Shetland Islands of Scotland, would buy knotted strings from old women. These strings were believed to have the magical power to control the winds. The more knots a sailor untied, the stronger the winds would blow for him.

Ladders

The unluckiness of walking under ladders has been attributed to the fact that condemned men walked beneath the ladder that led up the scaffold before they climbed it. Walking under a ladder is supposed to foretell death by hanging. The bad luck can be broken by spitting through the ladder, or else, spitting over your left shoulder, immediately afterward.

Other misfortunes have come to be associated with walking under a ladder: for example, an unmarried woman who does it will always be a spinster.

Mirrors

Some people believe that mirrors should be covered in a house where someone has just died, so that their soul's journey to heaven will not be hindered.

A mirror falling and breaking, for no discernible reason, is an ill omen that there will soon be a death in the house.

Breaking a mirror is widely believed to bring seven years' bad luck. But it's possible to remedy this disaster. Do not look into the broken mirror, and take the fragments out of the house. Bury the pieces or, better still, wash them in a stream that flows south to counteract the bad luck.
It is also believed unlucky by some to see your face in a mirror by candlelight.

The superstitious believe that a mirror attracts lightning, so that during a thunderstorm it should be covered.

Stairs

It is well known that it is bad luck to pass someone else on the stairs. But you should not change your mind and turn around on the stairs: continue up or down as the case may be. Some people would rather retrace their steps backward, if they need to return down the stairs because they have remembered something they should have brought with them.

Stumbling when you are going upstairs is good luck—the sign of a wedding coming soon; stumbling when coming down is bad luck.

Knitting

Sticking knitting needles through balls of yarn will bring bad luck to those who later wear the garments made from that yarn.

Knitting a pair of socks for a lover will have unhappy consequences: he will leave you—as could be foreseen from the fact that socks are garments made for walking. So make him some other garment, and you knit one of your own hairs into it, to bind him to you.

Do not start to knit clothes for your future children until you are pregnant. To do otherwise will bring bad luck: either you will have no child, or the child will be born sickly.

Sharp Things

Inadvertently crossing knives on a table means that there will soon be a quarrel in the house.

Once a pocket knife has been opened, it should be closed only by the person who opened it.

Some say that if you drop a pair of scissors, it means your lover is being unfaithful to you. However, if the scissors fall with both points sticking into the floor, it is a lucky omen: it means more work is coming to the household. If only one point sticks in, it means a death is coming.

In addition, scissors should never be picked up by the person who dropped them. (A similar belief is held concerning dropped gloves.) If there's no one else around, you can tread on them before picking them up, and ward off the bad luck that way. Be sure to close them before picking them up.

Scissors are regarded as unlucky gifts, because they can cut the ties of friendship or love. There is a simple way to deal with the situation if some well-meaning person, unaware of the danger, gives you scissors. Give a small coin (a "luck-penny") in return, and it is no longer a gift, but a purchase.

A slightly different practice has been dignified by no less a personage than the British monarch. In the past, when Queen Elizabeth has opened some building or function by cutting a ribbon, she has been known to hand the scissors back to the organizers together with a small coin, to neutralize the ill effect of passing a sharp object to another person.

Don't bother to keep searching in vain for some lost item: stick a pin into a cushion, say "I pin the Devil," and you can expect to find the object quickly.

Nails

A nail, unlike scissors or mirrors, is considered to be a lucky item. It's lucky, for example, to find one. If you have the good fortune to find one, you can keep it in your pocket as a charm.

You can find out whether someone is a witch by driving a nail into a footprint they have left. A witch is compelled to return and draw out the nail: an ordinary person will, of course, be unaware of what you've done.

Old writers tell of curing toothache by scratching the gum of the affected tooth with a new nail until the gum bled. The nail was then driven into a tree.

Hammering a nail into the wood over a door was also believed to protect the people in the house from toothache.

Coal

A very widespread belief is that carrying a piece of coal will bring luck. It doesn't harm its efficacy to wrap it in cloth or paper, and that will certainly help your clothes. It has always been thought unlucky, when one stirred the fire, to turn the coals over.

Hay

Many think it is bad luck to encounter a load of hay while traveling. However, some think it is only seeing the back of the load that is unlucky, and that it is good luck to see the hay approaching you.

Colors

To protect yourself from witches, wear a blue bead. Blue is also considered to be lucky; consider the rhyme:

> "Touch blue and your wish will come true."

Red is said to be a lucky charm against illness. For example, the health of a child, who has recently been sick, can be guarded by having them wear a red ribbon.

Beds

It's bad luck to put a hat on a bed.

If you make a bedspread, or a quilt, be sure to finish it or marriage will never come to you.

Placing a bed facing north and south brings misfortune.

You must get out of bed on the same side that you get in it or you will have bad luck.

When making the bed, don't interrupt your work, or you will spend a restless night in it.

Changing the bed on Friday will cause bad dreams.

Money

Some money superstitions seem to derive from our forebears' burning concern with thriftiness. The slightest carelessness with money would bring ruin, they suggest, and conversely, each small act of carefulness would be rewarded. Hence such rhymes as:

> "Find a penny, pick it up,
> All day long you'll have good luck."

"Money on the floor,
More at the door."

and such beliefs as:

Putting the first penny you receive each day into your pocket will attract more throughout the day.

Tossing a penny overboard while on a sea voyage will ensure a safe trip.

If you give a purse or wallet to someone, put a penny in it for good luck.

Some say that it's bad luck to pick up a coin if it's tails side up, but naturally it becomes lucky if it's heads side up.

You may think instead that it's always lucky to find a coin. But it's especially so if you find one with the year of your birth on it; keep it as a lucky charm.

Umbrellas

Opening an umbrella indoors is notoriously unlucky. Opening the umbrella over your head intensifies the harm.

But some think that the bad luck follows only if the umbrella is black. Others think it's unlucky only when the umbrella is opened without it first having been outdoors. And still others think it is bad luck only for a sick person in the house.

Furthermore, according to some, dropping an umbrella on the floor means that there will be a murder in the house in the near future.

Some people even believe that borrowing someone else's umbrella is bad luck.

Stones

You should not count the standing stones at Stonehenge; nor at other ancient mystical sites where there are standing stones (or henges). Or if you do, you will have bad luck.

A stone with a hole in it is lucky. If you find one with two holes, better still. In the past householders often hung them on ribbons over the door, and people would carry them to ward off bad luck in general and rheumatism in particular.

Cradles

If you rock an empty crib, it will have another occupant before the year is out.

The cradle must be paid for before it enters the house, or the child that lies in it will encounter extreme poverty at the end of its life, and will be buried in an unpaid-for coffin.

Jewelry

Piercing the ears for earrings is widely believed to be good for the eyesight. Seamen also believed that their earrings protected them from drowning.

To predict the sex of a baby. Suspend a wedding band held by a piece of thread over the palm of a pregnant woman. If the ring swings in an oval or circular motion the baby will be a girl. If the ring swings in a straight line the baby will be a boy.

Thirteen

The traditional fear of this number is said to derive from the fact that 13 people were present at the Last Supper. It manifests itself in many ways even today.

Friday 13 is well-known as a day of bad luck and there are several horror movies that use it in the title, and as a premise on which to base the plot. Many organizations also bow to the fear by designing their buildings in such a way as to avoid this number:

- Tall buildings often have no floor numbered 13.
- There is frequently no room 13 in hotels or hospitals.

Teeth

Gaps between teeth may not look very nice, but they are a happy omen of prosperity in life—specifically, that one would marry riches.

Dreaming about losing teeth is a sign that some friend or relative will die soon.

You must not dispose of a first tooth carelessly when it comes out: a dog might eat it, and you would find a dog-tooth growing in its place. Worse yet, it might fall into the hands of some malevolent person, who would be able to use it to cast a spell on the hapless child from whom it came.

In the past women would even keep the old teeth in long hair at the back of the head as a lucky charm. It was more usual to burn the tooth, but only after putting salt on it. Nowadays, of course, such teeth are entrusted to the Tooth Fairy.

Hair

Red-haired people have suffered much prejudice in the past. Red hair in a new child was supposed to indicate infidelity by the mother. It is supposed to be unlucky to meet a red-haired person first thing in the morning, and they should not be the first person across the threshold on New Year's Day. Possibly the prejudice grew up among the English at the time when they were in frequent conflict with the Scots.

Be careful not to drop your comb while combing your hair: it is an omen of a coming disappointment.

Throwing away one's cut hair, or the hair brushed from one's head, is as perilous as parting with anything else from one's body or clothing. Evil spells can be worked against one with the aid of one's hair, or alternatively a bird might use it to make its nest, which will condemn the former owner to constant headaches.

Anything lost from the body can be used in magic, affecting that person for good or ill. A hair from the head of a person with a cough can be used to cure their ailment. Put it between two slices of buttered bread, feed it to a dog, and chant:

> "Eat well, you hound,
> May you be sick and I be sound."

Don't pull out those gray hairs. If you do, ten will grow again in the place of each.

A double crown generally means good luck. The luck can take various forms: some say you are safe from drowning; others that you won't die in the country of your birth; others that you will eat your bread (that is, live) in two countries.

Fire

At Christmas or on New Year's Day, to help a neighbor to light a flame of any kind by giving them a light from your own fire or a candle will bring bad luck for the next year. Nor must you do it at any time when someone sick is in the room, for you are diminishing their life-strength by doing so.

Water

When the tide is flowing fast (that is, midway between high and low tides), water boils faster and butter forms more quickly in the churn.

In England, children suffering from whooping-cough were once taken to the shore at high tide. The ebbing tide was thought to take their cough away with it.

If you "make a face" (grimace) when the tide is turning, the ugly expression will be forever fixed on your face—just as it will if the wind changes direction.

Rivers

To cure stomach pains, gather 12 stones from 12 south-running rivers. If you place these under your mattress at night, they will cure your condition.

A cure for whooping cough is said to be to take porridge made over a south-running stream.

Rivers are traditionally regarded as being ruled by unfriendly spirits. In north-east England, Peg Powler was the spirit of the Tees. Jenny Greenteeth was a fairy who dwelt in several rivers in Lancashire, in northwest England.

Some rivers were regarded as bloodthirsty, and so had to be placated in various ways. An animal would be sacrificed to the River Ribble in northwest England, so that the fairy who was the spirit of the river would not take a human life, which she was liable to do every seven years. The River Dart, in the southwest, inspired this rhyme:

> "Dart, Dart cruel Dart, Every year thou claim'st a heart."

Usefully, if you are trying to escape from a witch, try to cross a river—apparently they are unable to cross running water.

Drowning

Traditionally it was unlucky to save a stranger from drowning. A proverb said: "Save a stranger from the sea, He shall be thy enemy." This was a particularly firmly held belief on the coasts of the English West Country, where whole villages lived on what they could salvage from wrecks, and often deliberately caused the wrecks themselves. They were not disposed to save the lives of those whose property they wished to gain.

The custom of throwing a coin into a fountain to bring good luck is still widespread. But formerly a wide variety of metal objects, from swords to pins and buttons, might be thrown into fountains and wells for the same purpose. Often this would be done as a kind of payment when taking the waters of a well or spring for their curative properties. A well at which this practice was favored would be called a "pin well" or "pen well."

When tossing a penny into a well, some believe that the correct way is to throw it over your left shoulder.

There are magical wells that foretell the future. At Oundle, England, the Drumming Well sometimes predicts disasters by emitting a loud rumble resembling a drum roll. The drying up of a well is usually regarded by local folk as a presage of evil. For example, St. Helen's Well in Staffordshire, England, foretold the outbreak of the English Civil War in 1642 by drying up. Another spring in Northamptonshire gives warning in the opposite way, by overflowing.

Holy Water

The water used in baptism is blessed by the priest. It is thought to have healing powers, but can also be misused by evil spirits or by devotees of Satan. Accordingly, some church fonts have covers that are kept locked when not in use.

On Ascension Day, Heaven was opened to receive the risen Christ. The rain that fell that day was thought to be especially holy, as having come direct from Heaven. Accordingly, rainwater and water from holy wells can be collected on that day and used for healing purposes and to bring good luck.

Young girls would once go out on May Day to wash their faces in the morning dew. Not only would the water improve their complexions but the girls had the opportunity to make a wish that they would be married within the year. The most curative dew was gathered from hawthorn, from ivy leaves, or from under an oak tree.

Holy Wine

Simple country folk, and even some more sophisticated people, have always believed that the things used in church services acquire a beneficent power by being associated with worship. They have sometimes stooped to theft to get their hands on these magical items so that they might help with some disease or malady of the mind.

Consecrated communion wine has been thought to be a great medicine for various ailments, including whooping cough in children, and priests have often been willing to allow it to be so used, though the official policy of the Church was against it.

People subject to epilepsy would creep under the communion table three times at midnight to be cured of their fits. Even sweepings from the floor beneath the altar were believed to be efficacious.

Christmas Superstitions

If you eat an apple on Christmas Eve, you will enjoy good health throughout the coming year.

And if you eat plum pudding at Christmas, you will avoid losing a friend before the next Christmas comes around.

If, before you eat anything else on Christmas morning, you eat a raw egg, you will ensure you will be able to carry heavy weights for the rest of the Yuletide season.

Visit plenty of friends at Christmas. In the coming year you will have as many happy months as the number of houses you eat mince pies in during this time.

If you refuse a mince pie when you are offered one at the Christmas dinner, the following day will be marked by bad luck.

Leave a loaf of bread on the table after dinner on Christmas Eve. This will ensure there is no lack of bread during the next year.

Snow at Christmas means that Easter will be green.

However, this might conflict with the belief that the weather on each of the 12 days of Christmas shows what the weather will be in the corresponding month of the coming year.

If Christmas Eve is clear, with star-filled skies, the summer will bring good crops.

A windy Christmas Day is supposed to bring good luck.

Many miraculous things are said to happen at midnight on Christmas Eve. All water turns to wine. Cattle kneel facing toward the east, and horses blow as if to warm the Christ child in the manger. Animals gain the gift of speech, though it is unlucky for a human being to hear them. Bees hum the Hundredth Psalm. However, don't presume to test any of these beliefs: it is bad luck to do so.

The child born on Christmas Day or Christmas Eve is believed in most countries to be especially lucky in its life. However, in Greece they fear that such a child is a wandering spirit. And in Poland they fear that the child may turn out to be a werewolf.

Some people believe that it is bad luck to wear new shoes on Christmas Day.

In Ireland it is believed that at midnight on Christmas Eve the gates of Heaven open. Those who die at that time go straight to Heaven, and are spared their stay in Purgatory.

You can make your fruit trees fruitful during the coming year by appropriate action on Christmas Eve. Tie wet bands of straw around them, or tie a stone to a branch.

It is said that nothing sown on Christmas Eve will die, even if the seed is sown in the snow.

The wise householder will guard the home's good luck by keeping a fire burning throughout the Christmas season. In fact, it is bad luck to let any fire go out in your house at this time.

Shoes should be placed side by side on Christmas Eve to prevent family quarrels.

During the Christmas season in Greece, some people burn their old shoes to prevent misfortunes in the coming year.

Beware if you find yourself in the Swedish countryside before the rooster crows on Christmas morning. The trolls (wicked elves) are said to roam about from cock-crow to dawn on that day.

In Devonshire, England, a girl who wants to know her marital prospects will rap at the henhouse door on Christmas Eve. If a rooster crows, she will marry within the next 12 months.

If you shout "Christmas Gift" to the first person who knocks on your door on Christmas Day, the visitor is bound to give you a present.

Never launder a Christmas present before you give it to someone, as this removes the good luck.

Place a cherry tree branch in water at the beginning of Advent. If it flowers by Christmas, you can be assured to receive lots of luck.

In the Netherlands people believe that if you take a fir stick, thrust it into the fire and let it burn partly, it will serve to ward off lightning if it is put under the bed.

Traditionally in England a special Yule candle had to burn in the house on Christmas Eve. Merchants would give large, specially made candles to their customers for this purpose, as they must be received as gifts, not purchased. They must not be blown out at bedtime, as the wick had to be preserved whole until the candle was burned out. So the candle was extinguished by carefully squeezing the wick with tongs.

Holly and ivy must both be included in Christmas decorations. The holly is lucky for the male members of the family, the ivy for the females.

Special Days

NEW YEAR'S DAY

The first water taken from a well or spring on New Year's Day has especially strong powers. Such water may bring health, or a good marriage, or general good luck.

GOOD FRIDAY

If you cut your hair on Good Friday, it is meant to prevent headaches in the forthcoming year.

A child who is born on Good Friday and baptized on Easter Sunday has a mystical gift of healing. If such a child is a boy, he should go into the Church.

Try to arrange your affairs so that you die on Good Friday: this is another of those holy days on which the dying are rewarded by going straight to heaven, without having to spend a period in Purgatory.

One should shed no blood on Good Friday, nor work with wood, nor hammer any nails; the symbolic relationship of all these to the events of the Passion is obvious.

DAYS OF THE WEEK

Friday and the week are seldom alike.
(The weather on Friday is usually different from that of the rest of the week.)

Friday night's dream on the Saturday told, is sure to come true, be it never so old.

Friday's hair and Saturday's horn go to the devil on Monday morn.
(It is unlucky to cut one's hair on Friday and one's nails on Saturday.)

Friday's moon, come when it will, comes too soon.
(A new moon on a Friday means bad weather.)

If you start a trip on a Friday, you will meet misfortune.

Don't start to make a garment on a Friday unless you can finish it the same day; otherwise it will always be unlucky.

Saturday's new, and Sunday's full, was never fine and never wool.
(A month in which the new moon falls on a Saturday and the full moon on a Sunday will have bad weather.)

Saturday is an unlucky day on which to begin new work. If you do so, you will find that there will be seven Saturdays before its completion. The belief was traditional in many different trades, including servants, farmers, and mariners.

It seems that almost any event or activity can be used to foretell one's luck according to the day of the week on which it occurs. For example, the day on which you find the first flower of spring:

"Monday: good fortune;
Tuesday: even the most ambitious attempts will be successful;

Wednesday: a marriage soon;

Thursday: a warning of bad luck in business;

Friday: wealth soon;

Saturday: misfortune;

Sunday: good luck for weeks."

One should also watch out for domestic disasters when hiring staff, as one superstition has it that Saturday's servants never stay, Sunday servants run away.

Weddings

Superstitions abound around weddings. Perhaps it's natural that, when two lives are joined, all involved wish they could somehow gain foreknowledge of the couple's future happiness or woe.

There are numberless superstitions about the bride's apparel:

The bride shouldn't help to make her own dress. And it is extremely unlucky to tear the dress on the wedding day, or to spill a drop of blood on it. It is unlucky to wear pearls as part of the bridal outfit.

Despite all these hazards, there are plenty of opportunities for the bride to encounter good luck. It's good luck to find a spider in the dress. The marriage is well favored if the bride should meet a lamb or a dove on her wedding day. If she kisses a chimney sweep, she will be lucky; even if he isn't her groom.

Among the bad omens for the wedding day are to see a pig, hare, or lizard running across the road; or an open grave; or meeting a nun or monk (the latter misfortune portends a childless marriage).

An old rhyme foretells the luck of a marriage according to the day of the week on which it takes place:

> "Monday for wealth
> Tuesday for health
> Wednesday the best day of all
> Thursday for losses
> Friday for crosses
> Saturday for no luck at all"

There are also more or less favorable times of the year at which to be married. They are summed up in this rhyme:

> "Married when the year is new,
> He'll be loving, kind, and true.
> When February birds do mate,
> You wed and do not dread your fate.
> If you wed when March winds blow,

Joy and sorrow both you'll know.
Marry in April when you can,
Joy for maiden and for man.
Marry in the month of May,
And you'll surely rue the day.
Marry when June roses grow,
Over land and sea you'll go.
Those who in July do wed
Must labor for their daily bread.
Whoever wed in August be,
Many a change is sure to see.
Marry in September's shrine,
Your living will be rich and fine.
If in October you do marry,
Love will come but riches tarry.
If you wed in bleak November,
Only joys will come, remember.
When December snows fall fast,
Marry and true love will last."

Roman Catholics have some extra weapons in their armory to help the success of the wedding. An image of the Virgin Mary placed in a window a week beforehand will help to guarantee a sunny day. Nevertheless if does rain on the morning of the ceremony, rosary beads hung from a window will help to send the rain away.

There seems to be little agreement about what the weather on a wedding day portends. According to some, raindrops at a wedding mean many teardrops during the marriage. According to others, they simply mean that there will be many children of the union. And others say that rain just means good luck.

The following rhyme gives just some of the rules that the superstitious bride will have to worry herself about:

"Married in white, you have chosen right,
Married in gray, you will go far away,
Married in black, you will wish yourself back,
Married in red, you will wish yourself dead,
Married in green, ashamed to be seen,
Married in blue, you will always be true,
Married in pearl, you will live in a whirl,
Married in yellow, ashamed of your fellow,
Married in brown, you will live in the town,
Married in pink, your spirit will sink."

If the bride cries on her wedding day, the marriage will never cause her any more tears supposedly.

A wedding during the time of day when the hour hand on the clock is going upward is lucky; when the hour hand is going downward, it's unlucky.

Traditionally the groom must not see the bride on the day of the wedding before she joins him at the altar. And he should not look over his shoulder to see her as she comes up the aisle to him. Both are considered to augur ill for the couple.

Dropping the wedding ring during the ceremony is a very unlucky omen: some say the marriage is doomed.

Rice thrown as the couple emerge from the church is intended to feed evil spirits, and distract them from disturbing the marriage.

And if any evil spirits are still lurking despite the rice throwing, the cans tied to the back of the newly married couple's car will frighten them away.

To avoid bad luck, the first gift opened by the bride should be the first one she uses.

One tradition says that the person who gives the third gift to be opened will soon have a baby themselves.

The single women who are guests at the wedding should keep their slice of wedding cake and keep it under their pillow. They will then assuredly dream of their future husband.

Stumbling on the threshold when entering the new home is a bad portent. Perhaps the custom of the groom carrying the bride over the threshold is designed to protect against this.

One of the most bizarre of wedding customs is to have a cat eat out of your left shoe a week before the wedding. This is supposed to bring you luck.

If ivy leaves representing two lovers are thrown onto a fire, their behavior shows the prospects for the relationship. If they jump together in the heat, the couple will marry; if they jump away from each other, the couple will part.

There will be a death in the parish soon if the church clock strikes during the sermon. If it strikes during the tolling of a funeral bell, there will be another funeral soon. A bride should wait outside the church rather than enter if the clock is likely to strike before the wedding service is over. It used to be thought in Wales that the town clock striking while the church bells were ringing was an omen of a fire.

Pregnancy and Child-raising

If any article of a new baby 's clothing is left in the home of a married woman, she will soon become pregnant.

If you want to know the size of your future family, look to see how many Xs you have in the palm of your right hand; that is the number of children you will have.

Twins

In Africa it is traditionally believed that twins are unlucky. They may be abandoned to die immediately after birth, and their mother may be killed as a witch.

In Britain it was often thought that if one twin dies, the survivor becomes stronger and acquires healing powers.

Christening

It used to be thought unlucky if a child did *not* cry at its christening. He or she would even be secretly pinched or slapped to make it cry. The reason was that the Devil is driven out at baptism, and will naturally cry out at that moment.

Boys must be baptized before girls at a christening; otherwise the boys will be beardless when they grow up and will envy the girls, for they will have beards.

Death

There is a grim superstition that babies born during the waning moon will not survive to adulthood.

And if a baby cuts its first teeth very early, it was once thought that it would die when still young.

There is an old superstition to the effect that "one funeral makes many": that is, that a death is likely to be followed by a spate of others.

In ancient times, weapons, utensils, food, and fine clothes would be buried with a corpse so that the deceased would be well provided for in the afterlife. Traces of the custom survived into the twentieth century: a coin was often placed in the mouth or hand of a corpse.

However, in many parts of England it was thought sacrilegious to bury someone with any of their jewelry or other valuables.

At gypsy funerals it was customary to smash the dead person's possessions, burn their caravan, and even kill their horses; all to ensure the welfare of the dead person in the life hereafter.

In Britain, and in parts of France, it was once believed that a dead person had the task of watching the graveyard until the next person to be buried took over. It was the watcher's task to guard the graves and to summon the next person to die.

In an alternative version of the belief, the first person to die in a year had this responsibility for the rest of the year. The watcher would ride the country roads in a ghostly horse-drawn cart, which could be heard but not seen. They would stop at the door of the next doomed person, and take their soul away. Sometimes funeral parties would fall to fighting with each other in the attempt to get their own departed one buried first, so that he or she would be spared this twelve-month delay in passing on.

When the soul leaves the body at the moment of death, it is said to be visible as a faint flamelike light. Such corpse-lights or corpse-candles have been reported flickering over the graves of the recently deceased. The tradition goes back at least to the time of the Icelandic sagas.

In other traditions, the lights are seen traveling from the churchyard to the house where someone is about to die. Here they are said to be the souls of the dying person's kin coming to summon him or her to join them.

If you are struck by lightning, your best chance of recovery will come if someone has the wit to bury you up to your neck in the ground.

In Ireland, a plaster made from mud scraped from the threshold of a house, and applied to the chest, was held to have special powers to cure fevers. The threshold is a place where blessings are traditionally uttered by those entering, and they're supposed to impregnate the ground.

There is a very widespread belief that it is unlucky to light three cigarettes from one match. It is often supposed that this superstition dates from the First World War, but in fact it was prevalent among soldiers in South Africa during the Boer

War (1899–1902). They thought that lighting the first cigarette at night would attract the attention of a sniper in the enemy trench, and lighting the second would give him time to take aim; he would fire as the third man's cigarette was lit. This seems to be the modern version of an ancient superstition that it is unlucky to light three candles from a single taper.

A superstition that goes back to the earliest days of photography is that, when three people are photographed together, the one in the middle will die first.

When someone dies, all the windows in the room should immediately be opened, to enable the soul of the deceased to make a speedy exit.

Furthermore, all doors in the house should be unlocked, for the same reason.

Generations of children have firmly believed that they must hold their breath while passing a cemetery, lest they breathe in the spirit of someone who has recently died and not yet passed on to the other world.

Bad luck will come your way if, when someone dies, you do not stop the clock in the room.

It is unlucky to bury a woman in black: she is liable to return to haunt the family.

Nor should a corpse's eyes be left open: it is said that he or she will then find someone "to take with them" that is, who will themselves soon die.

Cover the mirrors in a house in which there is a dead body: otherwise the next person to see their own reflection will die soon.

Yet another superstition pertinent to the conduct of funerals is: never hold one on a Friday. This portends another death in the family during the year.

Bad luck can assault the superstitious if they make any mistakes at a funeral:

- It's bad luck to count the cars in a funeral cortege.
- It's bad luck to meet a funeral procession head-on.
- Nothing new should be worn to a funeral, especially new shoes.
- Do not point at a funeral procession: this brings the danger that you will die within the month.
- Pregnant women should not attend funerals.

There is one superstition that lightens the gloom, however. Thunder following a funeral means that the dead person's soul has reached heaven.

If the person buried had lived a good life, flowers will grow on the grave. If their life was bad, weeds will grow. Perhaps conscientious relatives have sometimes taken care to tend a grave because they did not want to risk seeing the weeds spring up, damaging the posthumous reputation of a loved one.

It was once the custom in England to ask any visitor to a house where a death had just occurred to view the dead person and touch their corpse. Failure to do so was thought to prevent dreams of the deceased, or encourage possible hauntings. The practice is obviously dangerous when the death is due to infectious disease.

It was once thought that the corpse of a murder victim would bleed if touched by its murderer. Many people have been hanged on this evidence.

If the coffin has to be turned round on its journey to the burial, it is very bad luck, signifying that there will soon be another death in the family.

Nails or screws from a coffin that has been used to inter someone, or the handle of the coffin, can be used to make a lucky ring.

A piece of the wood of a coffin can be carried with one as a lucky charm.

Ghosts

You can protect your home from ghosts by removing a door and hanging it with the hinges on the other side.

It was also once common in England and Ireland to draw patterns on the doorstep with an unbroken line of chalk to keep ghosts out.

Yet another protection is to lay a poker on top of the fire, so that it forms a cross with the top bar of the grate, which will be visible to any evil spirit thinking of entering via the chimney.

Plants

An acorn should be carried to bring luck and ensure a long life.

An acorn at the window will keep lightning out.

The forked root of the mandrake makes the plant resemble a human figure, and a huge amount of legend and superstition has become associated with the plant. It is supposed to cure sterility in both human beings and animals, and also to have aphrodisiac powers. It can also help seers to divine the future. Some believe that, while living, it glows in the dark. In addition when pulled from the earth, it utters a shriek that causes anyone who hears it to go mad or drop dead. To pull it up safely, you have to tie a hungry dog to the plant, drop some meat just out of the dog's reach, and get out of harm's way before the dog uproots the plant.

The fruit of the mandrake is called the mandrake apple. Held in the hand last thing at night, it induces sleep.

If you cut an ordinary apple in half and count how many seeds are inside, you will apparently be able to divine how many children you will have.

Think of five or six names of someone you might marry. As you twist the stem of an apple, recite the names until the stem comes off. You will marry the person whose name you were saying when the stem fell off.

To give a child a long life, he or she is passed through the branches of a maple tree. Dreaming of marigolds is a sign of coming wealth.

We have all used a dandelion that has gone to seed to tell the time: the number of puffs needed to blow all the seeds away tells you what o'clock it is. Another superstition has it that, if you take a deep breath and blow away the seeds, the number that remain on the stem is the number of children you will have.

Thyme is especially associated with the dead. If the scent of thyme lingers around a place where the plant is not growing, it is a sign that a murder has been committed there.

The plant is supposed to fortify the spirits of those who use it as a medicine, however: it has traditionally been used as a remedy for melancholy.

All clover is regarded as lucky; but the four-leafed clover is, of course, especially so. When you find one, you will be able to see fairies and detect the presence of witches. Traditionally a four-leafed clover would be hidden in cow-sheds or dairies to protect the milk. An unmarried girl should wear the leaf in her right shoe: the first man she meets will be the one she marries (or, in some versions, someone of the same name).

It is unlucky to give or be given parsley. If your friend wants some from you, let her know that she must take it without your knowledge.

Parsley should not be transplanted: sow a new bed of it if necessary. And note that where parsley grows best is when the woman is the master in the house.

The fern called moonwort has the reputation of loosening anything assembled from iron components. Put into keyholes, it will undo the locks; if horses ride over it where it grows, it will loosen the nails in their horseshoes.

Mistletoe traditionally confers fertility. If a bough of mistletoe was laid next to the first cow that calved in the New Year, it would help the whole herd to multiply. Taken in a drink, it would help people to have children. Hence comes the custom that couples kiss beneath it at Yuletide celebrations. Any girl who did not get kissed under the mistletoe would not get married during the following year. At each kiss one of the berries is supposed to be plucked from the plant, and when the berries have all gone, the kissing has to stop. Some hold that the mistletoe must be burned after Christmas, or else those who have kissed under it will become enemies.

Some people are extremely superstitious about onions. They throw the peelings of the onion away immediately, and do not keep a cut onion around. Small onions are the most convenient for these nervous cooks.

St. John's wort is a lucky charm against the Devil, who cannot approach closer than nine paces to anyone carrying it. Naturally enough, its powers are greatest when gathered on St. John's Eve, the day before midsummer's day. Similar powers are ascribed to verbena, or vervain.

Lettuce is supposed to be bad for fertility. Having too much of it in the garden will reduce the number of children that the wife will bear and indeed, the husband's ability to beget them.

Keep witches at bay by planting rosemary by your doorstep.

Holly is believed to be lucky. Many people keep a sprig of it in the house all year around, not just at Christmas. Keeping a tree growing near a house also provides protection for the inhabitants.

Ivy is lucky for the house it grows on. If the ivy withers, it betokens bad luck. Birch brings good luck to any house that it decorates, and it was also worn in a buttonhole or on a hat for good luck. It is used to decorate houses on summer festivals, such as Whitsuntide or May Day. Birchwood crosses defend a house or farm buildings, such as pigsties, against evil spells.

Warts can supposedly be healed by digging up a turf, laying it back top-down, and reciting a spell. The wart would shrink with the withering of the grass on the inverted turf.

The Moon

The monthly cycle of the moon's phases is associated by many peoples with the monthly cycles of women, and hence with pregnancy and birth. In Greenland, it used to be believed that the moon was really a young man who paid night-time visits to any woman who chanced to sleep on her back. A girl who stared at the moon was likely to become pregnant.

The peasants of Brittany, in northwest France, believe that a pregnant woman, who exposes her skin to moonlight may give birth to monsters.

A tribe in Borneo believes that albinos owe their fair coloring to their father, who is the moon.

More generally, it is widely believed unlucky to point at the moon.

The new moon should be greeted respectfully. In some places men doffed their hats, or bowed, while women curtsied. You should turn over your money, without taking it out of your pocket. The Scots would carry a special coin with them, to be turned over three times when the new moon appeared. If you didn't have any money with you when you first noticed the new moon, your only recourse was to turn head over heels.

It is believed to be unlucky to see the new moon for the first time through glass. It is also unlucky to see it for the first time on the left hand or over one's shoulder.

Plants should be sown with due regard for the phase of the moon. Many kinds of seed should be sown when the moon is waxing (growing); some should be sown just after the full moon. Trees should be pollarded while the moon is waxing, so that their branches will grow straighter.

The rays of moonlight are supposed to make carcasses decay faster, which many a hunter has used to explain why he no longer has all the game he claims to have bagged at night.

Until late into the nineteenth century, the guardians of the royal forests of France were under orders to fell oaks only when the moon was waning, to ensure that the timber was of the best possible quality.

Apples must not be picked when the moon is waning, lest they shrivel up.

Even weather affecting the appearance of the moon can affect agriculture. According to Chinese tradition, if on the night of the fifteenth day of the eighth month (mid-fall), there were clouds obscuring the moon before midnight, it was a sign that oil and salt would become very dear. If there were clouds over the moon after midnight, the price of rice would undergo a similar change.

Sometimes we can see "the old moon in the arms of the new" (that is, the disk of the moon glimmering faintly, edged by the bright crescent of the new moon). This is reckoned a sign of fine weather; and so is the "turning up" of the horns of the new moon that is, the crescent being strongly tilted. In this position it is supposed to retain the water that is imagined to be in it, and which "would run out if the horns were turned down."

Sailors have long believed that when a star can be seen "dogging" the moon, then violent gales can be expected.

Rats will eat poison more readily when the moon is waxing.

Pigs should not be slaughtered when the moon is waning, for then their meat will also shrink when cooked.

Anything cut when the moon is waning will grow again but only slowly. So get your hair cut then if you wish to keep it short, and attend to the corns on your feet for prolonged comfort.

Births of animals and people, and marriages, will be unlucky if they occur during the waning moon.

Sleeping in moonlight was widely believed in Britain to cause blindness, or lunacy (the word "lunacy" comes from the Latin *luna,* meaning "moon"), or a swollen face.

The flow of blood in the human body was once thought to increase with the waxing of the moon. The once popular practice of blood-letting could be carried out safely only when the moon was waning.

You can cure warts by blowing on them nine times when the moon is full.

There is reputed to be a rock on a Scottish island in which there is a hollow, within which lies a stone called the Lunar Stone. This, unaided by human hand, "advances and retires according to the increase and decrease of the moon" that is moves forward and back according to the phase of the moon.

The Stars

Many think it is just as unlucky to point at the stars as at the moon. And it is also tempting fate to try to count the stars.

The song in Walt Disney's *Pinocchio* tells us that "when you wish upon a star, makes no difference who you are..." the wish is bound to come true. But more traditionally a shooting star has always been thought an evil omen, foretelling a death.

You don't have to wait for a shooting star to make a wish. An old rhyme says:

> "Star light, star bright,
> First star I see tonight,
> I wish I may, I wish I might
> Have the wish I wish tonight."

Eclipses

An ancient Indian belief is that when the sun or moon is eclipsed, a serpent or demon is eating the heavenly body concerned. It is said there are still many Hindus who believe that a demon is attempting to devour them.

The moon usually turns a deep red during an eclipse, an effect of the refraction by the earth's atmosphere of the red part of sunlight into the shadow in which the moon is enveloped. Some Native American peoples speak of the moon in eclipse as being hunted by huge dogs, which tear at her flesh until she is reddened by the blood flowing from her wounds.

Given these beliefs, it's natural to come to the assistance of the sun or moon by making a confused noise with all kinds of instruments. Various people from across many cultures think the noise will make the dragon or other monster loosen his grip and take to flight.

Among tribes from Peru to the Arctic, it was the custom to beat their dogs during an eclipse. They explained this by saying that the big dog was swallowing the sun and by whipping the little ones they could make him stop.

The Chinese ascribed eclipses of both sun and moon to the machinations of a dragon. It was a part of the official duties of mandarins to "save the sun and moon when eclipsed." The imperial astronomers at the capital would inform the Board of Rites of the precise time of a forthcoming eclipse, and this body would inform the

viceroys or governors of the 18 provinces of the empire. These and their subordi-
nate officers would make arrangements to save the moon or the sun at the appoint-
ed time, by means of praying, burning incense, lighting candles, and making loud
noises on instruments.

Eclipses had a further meaning to the Chinese. If a sovereign were remiss in government, Heaven would terrify him with calamities and strange portents. These
were divine reprimands sent to recall him to a sense of duty. Eclipses of the sun
and moon were "manifest warnings that the rod of empire was not wielded aright."
These ceremonies continued long after the educated classes had learned from
Western missionaries the true causes of eclipses.

Similar practices continued in remote parts of Italy and elsewhere in Europe until
medieval times. The belief here was that the noise would drown out the spells of
witches, so that the moon or sun would not hear them.

Christopher Columbus greatly benefited from his knowledge of astronomy and the
superstition of the Native Americans. In 1504 he and his men were being kept prisoner by the local people, and were close to starving. He threatened to take away
the light of the moon if they did not bring them food. They refused, but were intimi-
dated when on March 1 the moon disappeared as Columbus had foreseen. They
brought food and pleaded for his pardon.

Birds

When you first hear the cuckoo, you should turn over the money in your pocket. This is supposed to ensure good financial luck throughout the following year. Ideally you should be standing on something soft, such as grass or moss, or else the coming year will not be prosperous and comfortable for you.

Some country people used to believe that if the song-thrush (also called the mavis) built its nest unusually high in the thorn-bush, there was something wrong in fairyland. When the fairies had their affairs in proper order, they would always see to it that the nests were built near the ground, so that they could enjoy the beautiful song of the thrush.

According to legend, the crops of blackbirds hold the souls of those who must remain in purgatory until Judgment Day. When the birds sing unusually sweetly, we are hearing the thirsty souls crying out for rain.

The Tower of London has been home to ravens for centuries. It is said that if they ever leave, the Tower will fall and disaster will befall England. Of course, no one really believes this, but the British government takes care that there are always at least six ravens in residence, just to be on the safe side.

The direction from which you hear a bird calling is supposed to be of significance in foretelling the future. This belief seems to derive from divination by the movements of birds, as practiced in ancient Rome.

- To hear a bird calling to the north means some serious misfortune involving death or injury;
- A bird calling in the south signifies a good harvest;
- One calling from the west is good luck;
- One calling from the east signifies love.

Even having bird droppings land on you or on your nicely polished car is not the misfortune it seems. Many people believe that it is actually good luck.

The first bird that an unmarried girl sees on St. Valentine's Day will give her a clue to her future husband:

- If it's a robin, he'll be a sailor.
- If it's a blackbird, he'll be a clergyman.
- If it's a crossbill, he'll be a bad-tempered fellow.
- If it's a woodpecker, the girl will stay unmarried.

Seeing a bird is generally considered good luck, but some are associated with bad luck. It is good luck to watch a hawk hunt, or to see swallows, hummingbirds, wrens, or robins. But it can be bad luck to see crows or swifts, or even an owl by daylight.

An old legend says that the robin tirelessly flies back and forth between our world and hell, carrying water in its beak to moderate the flames. Because it is accustomed to the heat of hell, it feels the cold of winter more than other birds, which is why it shivers so much. In the course of its flights of mercy, its feathers are singed, giving it the red breast.

But according to another legend, the robin got its red breast when it plucked a thorn from the crown of Christ on the Cross, attempting to alleviate his sufferings, and some of the holy blood fell onto the bird. But according to either tale, it is very bad luck to harm such a noble creature.

You should make a wish on seeing the first robin of spring. Make sure you complete the wish before the bird escapes, taking the power of the wish with it.

The wren is the wife of the robin, and in some places it is considered bad luck to harm her for this reason. Yet in other places the wren used to be hunted on certain days. On the Isle of Man, off the northwest coast of England, the wren-hunt took place on Christmas Eve and St. Stephen's Day. The wren was there regarded as being an evil fairy who had lured many men to destruction, but had assumed the form of a wren to escape punishment.

It was once thought that barnacle geese, which are Arctic birds somewhat smaller than the familiar domestic geese, hatched out from barnacle shells. Those that fell into water when they hatched grew into the adult birds; those that hatched out on land died. The belief may have arisen because of a confusion over an earlier name for the bird, Hibernicula, meaning "of Hibernia (Ireland)."

The croaking of a raven portends death.

But don't be tempted to harm a raven: it might house the soul of the legendary King Arthur, revisiting the world of mortals.

When you see magpies while out walking, an old rhyme tells you their meaning:

> "One for sorrow, two for mirth;
> Three for a wedding, four for a birth;
> Five for silver, six for gold;
> Seven for a secret, not to be told;
> Eight for heaven, nine for hell;
> And ten for the Devil's own self."

According to an old story, a solitary magpie is so unlucky because it was the only bird that refused to enter the Ark with Noah. You can counter this by repeating "Good morning Mr Magpie" three times, then asking "How is your wife and family?" when you encounter a single bird.

A very similar rhyme is usually associated with counting crows:

> "One's bad, Two's luck,
> Three's health, Four's wealth,
> Five's sickness, Six is death."

Some cultures have thought owls were wise, and that a man could increase his knowledge by killing and roasting one. The ancient Greeks, too, associated owls with wisdom, and linked them to Athena, the goddess of wisdom and learning. They therefore held owls to be sacred.

Elsewhere, the owl was viewed as sinister. In some countries in Eastern Europe, to hear the hoot of an owl was very unlucky. To rid yourself of the bad luck and counter any evil spirits, superstition required that you undress immediately, turn your clothes inside out and put them back on. The fact that owls tend to hoot only at night usually protected the modesty of citizens.

The owl was regarded by the citizens of ancient Rome as so unlucky that, when one flew into the Capitol in the heart of the city, the whole of Rome had to be purified in a special ceremony.

If you hear an owl hooting and want to counteract the bad luck that this brings, throw peppers, vinegar, or salt into the fire. This will make the tongue of the distant owl sore and it will fly away, leaving you in peace.

Martins and swallows are both regarded as lucky birds, as shown in the old rhyme:

> "The martin and the swallow
> Are God Almighty's birds to hallow."

The feathers of the peacock, marked with conspicuous and rather frightening "eyes," are supposed to be very unlucky particularly if brought indoors.

The Romans used to guide affairs of state by augury, or divination by birds. There was a body of officials called augurs, at first three in number, and eventually rising to 15. In one method, an augur, after sacrifice and prayer, would watch for the direction from which a bird would appear, its direction of flight, and call. Another method of divination involved feeding specially-kept chickens. If they fed hungrily, the omens were good; if they were off their food that day, the omens were bad.

The Germans used to say that the crossbill would always awaken a child that it found sleeping in moonlight, as this, it was thought, could cause lunacy or death.

Particular great families or important persons have had particular birds associated with them as harbingers of good or ill fortune:

- The Wardour family, of Arundel in England, would be warned of an imminent death by he sight of two white owls perched on a roof.
- It used to be believed in Sussex, England, that a heron would perch on Chichester Cathedral when the Bishop was about to die.
- The death of the Bishop of Salisbury is announced by the appearance of two large white birds in flight.

A dove or a white pigeon is a fortunate thing to see around someone who is about to die or has just died. It indicates that they will find happiness beyond the grave.

A nocturnal bird that is seen or heard by day is an unlucky omen.

Seagulls are a bad portent. If you see a trio of them together, flying directly overhead, there will be a death soon among those near to you.

If you don't see any jaybirds on Friday, the reason is simple. That's the day they go down to hell to tell the Devil all about the sinful activities they've seen during the week. If you *do* happen to see a jaybird that day, the reason is equally simple, he's the one who's stayed behind to make sure nothing is missed on this day either.

Animals

DOGS

Dogs are often believed to be capable of seeing ghosts. However, some people believe that only a dog with seven toes can do this.

If a dog howled outside the house of a sick person, it was thought to be an omen that the person would die. If the dog was driven away and returned to howl again, the omen was thought to be especially bad. An old rhyme sums up the fear about dogs howling:

> "Dogs howling in the dark of night
> Howl for death before daylight."

A black dog crossing your path is considered unlucky in most countries. It's especially unlucky if it follows you and won't be driven away.

Certain Sioux tribes believed that if a sick person shared their bed with a dog, the illness would be transferred to the animal.

In the past, dogs that had bitten someone were often killed. It was thought that if they were to develop rabies, the same disease would appear in the person they had bitten earlier.

If a rabid dog bit someone, the victim might have to eat some of the dog in order to prevent the disease developing.

CATS

For some reason, cats have attracted more than their fair share of superstition. But in different countries cats are viewed very differently: sometimes as objects of fear, sometimes as harbingers of good luck.

In the United States, it is unlucky to have a black cat cross your path. But if you hold back and let someone else go ahead of you, they may count as the person whose path has been crossed, and accordingly receive the bad luck. It's also possible to fend off the bad luck by taking 12 steps backward.

The Irish agreed that the black cat was unlucky; they were even more specific, and said that if it crossed your path by moonlight, you would die in an epidemic.

In America it's also traditionally good luck to see a white cat on the road, but bad luck to see it at night. But *dreaming* of a white cat is lucky.

In Britain, however, it is lucky to see a black cat. In Scotland, it specifically has to be a strange black cat, and on your porch.

English schoolchildren used to believe that seeing a white cat on the way to school was unlucky. The remedy was to spit, or else to turn right around, and make the sign of the cross.

In the old days in northern France, meeting a tortoiseshell cat foretold of death in an accident.

According to an old belief, cats must be kept away from babies because they "suck the breath" of the child.

On every black cat there is believed to be one white hair. If you can pull that hair from the cat without getting scratched, it will bring you good fortune in wealth and love.

In Bohemia, the cat was a symbol of fertility. When a cat died it was usually buried in the cornfields to give a good crop.

If an unmarried girl in the South of France steps on a cat's tail, she will meet her future husband within 12 months.

In mythology, the cat was believed to have great influence on the weather. Witches who rode on storms took the form of cats. The dog, an attendant of the storm king Odin, was a symbol of wind. Cats came to symbolize downpours of rain and dogs to symbolize strong winds. This may be how we got the phrase "it's raining cats and dogs."

When moving into a new home, you should always, according to an American superstition, put the cat in through the window instead of the door, so that it won't leave home and run off.

When a girl living in the Ozark Mountains received a proposal of marriage and was uncertain whether to accept, she folded three hairs from a cat's tail into a piece of paper and placed it under her doorstep. The next morning she would unfold the paper to see if the hairs had formed themselves into a Y or N before giving her answer.

A cat onboard a ship is considered to bring luck.

Sailors used cats to predict the luck they would meet on the voyages they were about to embark upon. Loud mewing meant that it would be a difficult voyage. A playful cat meant that it would be a voyage with good, strong winds. If a sailor's wife wanted to keep him at home, she only had to trap a cat under a tub or pot to make the weather unfavorable.

French peasants thought they could find buried treasure if they followed a specific ritual with a black cat. They would find an intersection where five roads met, then turn the cat loose and follow it.

In the past, many women have suffered because of the belief that if a cat ran over the body of a pregnant woman, she was likely to lose the child.

In ancient Egypt, cats were revered and were sacred to the goddess Isis. Embalmed cats were buried in the tombs of the great. Surprisingly, a similar sort of reverence may have prevailed in England, thousands of years later, for it was once the practice there to seal mummified cats in the walls of houses to ward off evil spirits.

Sacred cats kept in a sanctuary in ancient Egypt were carefully tended by priests who watched them day and night. The priests interpreted the cats' movements— the twitch of a whisker, a yawn or stretch—to make predictions of events that would happen in the future.

Cats would be locked away when someone had died, so that there was no risk of their jumping over the corpse. To do so would cause bad luck for someone in the household. In England, a cat on top of a tombstone was a sign that the soul of the departed was possessed by the devil. Two cats seen fighting near a dying person, or on the grave shortly after a funeral, were believed to be the Devil and an angel fighting for possession of the soul.

In the Netherlands cats were not allowed in rooms where private family discussions were going on. The Dutch believed that cats were sure to spread gossip around the town.

According to the Italians, it is good luck to hear a cat sneeze.

Elsewhere its is believed that if a cat sneezes close to the bride on the morning of her wedding it will be a happy marriage.

According to an American belief, if you see a one-eyed cat you should spit on your thumb, press the thumb into the palm of your other hand, and make a wish. The wish will come true.

An old belief is that a cat will not stay in the house when someone is about to die, so it's a bad omen if the cat leaves the house when someone is ill.

There is an English belief that a cat washing behind its ears means that it will soon rain. If a cat sleeps with all its paws tucked underneath itself, there is cold weather ahead.

According to a Welsh superstition, when a cat's pupil dilates, it means rain soon.

A kitten born in May was once believed to be so unlucky that it was likely to be drowned.

Black cats have always been regarded as the familiars (companions) of witches. It is said that a black cat that has served as the familiar of a witch for seven years itself becomes a witch.

TOADS AND FROGS

Toads are often thought of as the companions of witches, or else as a favorite ingredient in their potions. Toads are therefore often regarded as unlucky—but not always: it is lucky to encounter a toad, and killing one will bring on bad weather.

Perhaps because of its own warty skin, the toad has been regarded as having powers to cure skin afflictions. Closing a living toad in a bag hung round one's neck and allowing it to die there will cure warts and tumors and skin diseases.

The toadstone is an undistinguished-looking dark gray or light brown stone that was thought to come from the head of aged toads. They were carried or worn as lucky charms. They would change color if the owner were bewitched.

Warts can also be cured by frogs, but you have to rub the living animal on them.

A frog brings good luck to any house that it enters.

BATS

In China and in Poland, bats do not have the ominous connotations that they have in the West: if you see one at an auspicious moment, you can look forward to long life and happiness.

Bats have never been looked on so favorably in most of Europe and in America. According to one superstition, if a bat flies three times around a house, it is a portent of death.

Bats are regarded as being good weather forecasters. When bats come out before dark and flit about, it is a sign of good weather to come.

It's said that if a bat lands on your head, it won't get off until it hears thunder.

MOLES

Molehills appearing in a circle around a house portend a death in the family. If they don't form a circle they are luckier, for then they mean only that someone will be moving house soon.

Moles' feet are a cure-all for toothache and fever in children. They need to be hung around the patient's neck in a bag. Adult country people would often wear one on a watch-chain to guard against rheumatism.

RABBITS

The rabbit's foot is thought to be especially lucky when rubbed on the face of a child. It was formerly often placed in a child's baby carriage. The hare's foot is also regarded as lucky. Actors used to apply their make up with a rabbit's foot.

A rabbit that crosses the path in front of you bodes well; one that crosses behind you is a bad portent.

Rabbits have sometimes enjoyed a bad reputation because they dwell underground, like Old Nick himself.

MICE

A mouse squeaking near a sickbed is a fatal omen for the sick person. If mice suddenly abandon a house, or suddenly infest it, it is bad luck for those living there.

Mice were formerly cooked and eaten as cures for colds and fevers. Drinking water in which a mouse had been boiled was also a remedy for quinsy (an inflammation of the tonsils). To cure a persistent cough, you are recommended to wear a bag around your neck containing a whole nest of mice. Your cough will pass to them and disappear as they die.

Sometimes in the past, mothers would place their children's milk teeth, after they had fallen out, into a mousehole. In exchange, the child's new teeth would be small and sharp, like the teeth of a mouse.

CATTLE

The Icelanders say that If the first calf to be born during the winter is white, it presages a bad winter.

Cow's dung used to be pushed into the mouth of a new-born calf to give it lifelong protection against evil magic.

It was once thought that by living close to where cows were kept you'd never get tuberculosis.

It is unlucky to try to buy cattle that have not been offered for sale.

Cattle that stand close together, on low ground, are foretelling rain; they stand on high ground when the weather is to be fair.

If a plow should kill a daddy-longlegs, the cows in the herd will fail to give milk.

Certainly there must be some close affinity between the insects and the animals, because if you ask a daddy-longlegs, "Where are the cows?" it will point its antennas in the right direction—or so it is said.

SHEEP

It is good luck to meet a flock of sheep while you are traveling. but its worth noting also that restless sheep are an omen of bad weather..

Shepherds in some places believe that they must wash their eyes in running water before they will be able to count their sheep accurately.

Carry the bone from a joint of mutton with you as a lucky charm if you wish to ward off rheumatism.

In bygone days the sheep was not only a valuable domestic animal on which the prosperity of whole communities depended, a source of food and the raw materials of clothing, but also a rich source of charms and magical cures for all manner of disorders.

If your lungs were afflicted with pneumonia, the lung of a sheep could be applied to your feet, and the disease would go to the animal's lung in preference to yours.

If a child had whooping cough, it could be cured by the breath of a healthy sheep.

You would need to be wrapped in the whole skin of a newly killed sheep to cure an adder bite.

HORSES

Superstitions differ from country to country regarding the lucky or unlucky quali-
ties of white horses: in some places they are lucky, in others the opposite. When you encounter a white horse, you should spit and make a wish. Alternatively, you should cross your fingers until you see a dog.

Some country people still seek to bring luck to their house by leading a horse through it.

Parts of the body of a horse have traditionally been supposed to have curative pow-
ers. Horse-hairs, chopped and put into bread and butter, would be fed to children to cure worms. Similar beliefs about the hairs of other animals, including donkeys and dogs, have been prevalent in the past.

On the leg of a horse, horse-spurs often appear: these are calluses. A traditional remedy for cancer was to cut these off, dry them and grind them up, and take them in milk.

Horse-brasses, which were common before the displacement of the horse by the tractor for working the land, were both ornaments and lucky charms. They took the form of lucky shapes, such as rayed suns or crescent moons. Even when working, a horse would be adorned with a few brasses to provide protection from ill luck.

DONKEYS

On the back of the donkey is a cross consisting of dark hair. This is a vestige of the entry of Jesus into Jerusalem on a donkey's back. Needless to say, in the light of this tradition, hairs from this part of the donkey's back have been regarded as having beneficent powers. Worn as a charm, they cure or prevent various disorders.

Sometimes children would be required to ride a donkey, sitting facing backward, to prevent diseases such as measles.

Letting a black donkey share a field with pregnant mares will guarantee that they foal successfully.

To see a dead donkey is very lucky. To leap over it three times is luckier still.

WOLVES

Many superstitious beliefs gathered around the mysterious and feared wolf. Like other powerful predator animals, it yielded body parts that were especially prized in the pharmacies of the ancient apothecaries. Its liver was held to ease the pain of childbirth. Its paw, kept in a bag around one's neck, could heal throat infections.

One had to be careful riding where wolves had been: a horse could be crippled if it stepped into a wolf's paw-print.

Even to allow oneself to be gazed on by a wolf was to court blindness.

The early naturalists believed that wolves sharpened their teeth on stones before setting out hunting.

CHICKENS AND EGGS

Sailors in the past thought it unlucky to refer to eggs directly while at sea. It is supposed to be unlucky for anyone to dream of eggs, especially rotten ones.

In the past Easter eggs have been much more than toys or candies. A red-painted Easter egg would be planted in the fields in Europe to protect them from bad weather, and a decorated egg might be kept in the house as a good luck charm. An egg laid on Good Friday can be kept to serve as a good luck charm.

When eggs are "set" (placed) under a hen to incubate, there should be an odd number, or else they will not hatch or will all be roosters. They must not be set on a Sunday.

Double-yoked eggs are supposed to be unlucky.

Break the shell of a boiled egg after eating it: that will prevent witches from using it to travel in, over land or water. The same action also protects all sailors at sea.

But don't burn empty eggshells: that will stop the hens from laying.

A woman who heard a rooster crowing around the time her baby was born was doomed to ill luck. This belief was taken so seriously in some places that all the roosters in the area would be slaughtered when a baby was due.

Hens that roost in the morning portend a death in the household.

If a hen enters the house or a rooster crows near the door, a visitor will arrive soon.

When a rooster crows at midnight a spirit is passing.

If a rooster crows while perched on a gate the next day will be rainy. The same weather can be foreseen if it crows at nightfall.

A white rooster is very lucky, and should not be killed, as it protects the farm on which it lives.

INSECTS AND SPIDERS

If a bee enters your home, it's a sign that you will soon have a visitor. If you kill the bee, you will have bad luck, or the visitor will be unpleasant.

A bee-sting is not necessarily all bad luck: it is reputed to be able to prevent or cure rheumatism.

A swarm of bees settling on a roof is an omen that the house will burn down.

But if a bee settles on your hand, try not to be frightened: it is a portent that money is coming to you. And if the bee settles on you head, it's even better: it means you will achieve greatness.

However, a bee will attack you if you swear in its presence, or if you have been unfaithful in some way. In past times a sign of a girl's virginity, which few, surely, would have the courage to undertake, was her ability to walk through a swarm of bees unharmed.

Bees must be told all the news about the household of the keeper. The death of the keeper must be announced to them: someone close to the deceased person, such as the child or surviving partner, must rap on each hive three times, saying "The master is dead!" or else the bees will desert you. In the past hives were often draped with black crape as a sign of mourning.

Bees should not be bought, for then they will not flourish. The best chance that a swarm will do well is to have it given freely; otherwise it can be received in exchange for goods.

A ladybug is yet another creature that it is bad luck to harm. It can tell an unmarried girl something about her future husband: if she catches one and then releases it, it will fly off in the direction from which her future husband will come.

The more spots there are on a ladybug that lands on you, the luckier it is.

You'll be going on a journey soon if you catch sight of a spider running down its web in the afternoon.

A spider once hid the baby Jesus from the soldiers of Herod by weaving a web over him. That is why spiders are good luck now, and why some say it is unlucky to harm one.

But others are not averse to harming spiders in the cause of medicine: a little crushed spider in syrup is a remedy for fever. And If you shut a spider in a walnut shell that you hang around your neck, you will ward off the plague for as long as it's alive.

A moth flying around your lamp late at night portends the arrival of a postcard. If it makes two circuits of the lamp, there will be a letter; and if three, a parcel.

A moth or butterfly seen in the room of someone just dead is supposed to be the late person's soul. Needless to say, it is bad luck to kill it.

According to some, however, a white moth inside the house or trying to enter it means death.

"He who would wish to thrive must let spiders run alive," is an old proverb that reflects the widespread belief that it is unlucky to harm spiders.

In some places butterflies have been viewed favourably, as deserving protection. One old superstition regards butterflies as souls, lingering after the deaths of their owners. In some places they have been thought to be the souls of unbaptized children, which cannot enter Heaven.

In other places and times, butterflies have been unlucky. It is a bad omen to see three butterflies flying together. Sometimes it is said that the first butterfly to be seen in a year should be killed to avoid bad luck. Crushing the butterfly underfoot will enable you to crush your enemies.

However, if the first butterfly you see in the year is white, you will have good luck all year.

A cricket in the house singing its unmistakable song, brings good luck to everyone therein.

FISH

A dream of fish means that someone near to you is expecting a child.

Superstitious anglers think it's unlucky to get married at a time when the fish aren't biting.

Sleep and Dreams

An old rhyme runs:

> "Dreams at night, a devil's delight;
> Dreams in the morning, angels' warning."

This implies that we should be inclined to ignore dreams that we have in the night, which may be maliciously inspired by dark forces, but be ready to act on the warnings of dreams that we have just before waking.

If you see a lizard in your dreams, you are being warned that you have a secret enemy.

An old tradition is that we sleep best with our heads toward Jerusalem. For some, this traditional belief, with its clear religious inspiration, has been replaced by a more modern piece of "alternative medicine:" that the best position to sleep in is with your head to the north and feet to the south. The idea is that the north–south direction of the earth's magnetic field influences the functioning of the body.

The way to preserve the fidelity of your husband is to sew a swan's feather into his pillow.

The symbolism of dreams can be perverse. It is said that if you dream of death, it's a sign of a birth: if you dream of birth, it's a sign of death.

Dreams of acorns are portents of pleasant things to come. If a woman dreams of eating acorns, she will gain a comfortable position in the world, with ease and comfort in plenty.

If you dream of shaking acorns from a tree, it means that life will just as readily shower its rewards on you, in business affairs or in love.

Almonds merely seen in a dream portend a short-lived sorrow. If they are not only seen but enjoyed, the meaning of the dream depends on their taste. If they taste sweet, you'll be lucky; if they taste bitter, then changes that you plan in the near future are risky, and you should put them off for as long as possible.

To dream of angels is lucky: success, security, happiness and friendship are predicted.

Seeing a baby in a dream indicates all the warm and positive things that we associate with them: innocence and new beginnings. It signifies that you will make new friendships in the near future, perhaps even have a new love affair.

However, if a woman dreams that she is actually nursing a baby, it is a warning that she will be deceived by someone whom she greatly trusts.

Sometimes the symbolism of dreams is extremely clear. It is the fate of party balloons to end their lives with a spectacular bang or a slow deflation. Not surprisingly, therefore, seeing balloons in a dream signifies the dashing of hope in some enterprise, and failure in business. This gloomy prognosis applies even if you dream of ascending by hot-air balloon.

If you kill a bear in a dream, it signifies liberating yourself from some sort of constricting entanglement.

Dreaming of a freshly made bed with snowy white sheets signifies the early end of some worry that has been oppressing you.

A new lover in a woman's life will be foreshadowed by dreams of making a bed.

Riding a bicycle in a dream portends bright prospects when you are riding uphill, but can be a warning of imminent misfortune if you are riding downhill.

Dreams of birds in flight are portents of prosperity.

Dreams of butterflies on flowers indicates future prosperity. If the butterflies are flitting around, there will be a letter from an absent friend.

If candles seen in a dream are burning with a clear and steady flame, you are surrounded by trustworthy friends and kinsfolk, and your prosperity is securely founded. Dreams of cats are generally bad omens. They may be warnings of treachery or other misfortunes to come. However, if you dream of overcoming cats that attack you in a dream, it indicates that you will overcome obstacles in life and go on to new heights.

It is traditionally supposed to be a very bad omen indeed to see a crow in your dreams: it betokens nothing but grief and misfortune.

Dreaming that you are dancing is a good omen. It signifies that good fortune—something unexpected—is on its way to you.

While it seems only natural that one should spontaneously dream of near ones who are no longer living, the superstitious hold that such dreams may carry special meaning. They are held to come as warnings, and indicate that something is amiss in your life at the relevant time. If in your dream the dead person speaks to you specifically, what they have to say is of great importance.

Dreaming of diamonds is a sign as cheerful as one would hope and imagine: it signifies that you will be honored in the near future, with your merit being recognized by those in high places.

Dreaming about dogs suggests that your friends will be constant and true.

However, in dreams the barking of dogs indicates that bad news is on the way.

If you dream that a dragonfly lands on you, you will receive excellent news from someone who is far away from home. But if you see a dead dragonfly, then the news will be bad.

A dragonfly that is perching on some object indicates that you will soon be having guests—who may be hard to get rid of.

If in a dream you are driving a vehicle, it is a warning that you should take no chances with money in the near future.

If you dream that you are being driven in a vehicle by someone else, you will soon have some luck with money.

Dreaming of faces is rich in significance:

- a smiling face portends new friends and experiences, perhaps financial gains.
- an unpleasant, even grotesque, face indicates that there will be loss in your life soon.
- strangers' faces indicate that you'll soon be changing your place of residence.
- washing your face means that you are aware that you need to atone for past errors or wrongdoings.
- Dreaming of falling indicates a deep insecurity about one's ability to maintain self-control or control of one's situation.

If you dream of falling and being hurt, expect to go through hard times. If you dream of falling without being hurt, your reversals will be short-lived.

Not surprisingly, dreams of well-tended gardens are viewed by the superstitious as representing peace, security and all good things.

- A vegetable garden promises increased prosperity, provided only that you exercise due diligence and care.
- A flower garden foreshadows tranquility, comfort, love and a happy home.
- A neglected, overgrown garden represents your neglect of yourself and your own deepest needs.

Gloves in a dream represent troubles with business or the law. However, they are a hopeful sign, indicating that you will arrive at a settlement that benefits you.

Trades and Professions

SEAFARERS AND FISHERMEN

If you throw back the first fish you catch, you'll be lucky in your fishing for the rest of the day.

But if at any point you count the fish you've caught, you will catch no more that day.

A voyage begun on Friday will have bad luck.

Fishermen in the past often believed that it was unlucky to see a clergyman when they were on their way to their boats. Nothing to do with the church must be mentioned at sea. It was even more unlucky to have ministers on board a ship at sea.

It is equally unlucky to take a pin on board ship.

Sailors' womenfolk must not attend to their hair after nightfall, for it will bring harm to their loved ones at sea.

Icelanders have lived off the sea ever since the Vikings first settled there and so there are many superstitions relating to fishing. If a fisherman drops a knife while cleaning fish, and the knife points to the sea, there will be good fishing when the crew next go to sea. If, however, the knife points to the land, that will bring bad fishing when they next cast their nets. The moral of this story is clearly: if you're going to clean fish on the boat, do it a long way from land.

CHURCH PEOPLE

It is good luck to encounter nuns—but not if they are walking away from you.

In Cornwall it was believed that you could neutralize the bad luck that followed seeing a minister of the church if you immediately touched some iron.

PERFORMERS

You must never wish an actor good luck before a performance—that is sure to bring trouble on it. Instead, you must wish them bad luck by saying "break a leg!" The same superstition is held by sailors starting out on a voyage and to punters heading for the race-course.

It is bad luck to whistle a tune, or to applaud, backstage.

A production will be ill-omened if there is a mirror, or real flowers, onstage.

It is bad luck to say the last line of the play during rehearsals.

Even when not in use, the stage should always be illuminated by a "ghost light"—otherwise the production will come to an early end.

Shakespeare's tragedy *Macbeth* is notoriously regarded as unlucky to perform. Actors never mention it by name, calling it simply "the Scottish play."

Around the World

There is a 200-year-old superstition in Iceland that if you don't get at least one piece of new clothing to wear for Christmas, the Christmas Cat will come and get you. The Christmas Cat was a monster that originated from the other Nordic countries, but it is still spoken of today in Iceland. It provides the perfect excuse to go shopping.

In the Philippines they say that wearing polka dots on New Year's Eve will attract money and wealth in the future. The polka dots symbolize coins.

Another Filipino superstition is that you should throw open every door in the house as the new year begins and lay the table with round items of food—pies, cakes, fruits, and so on. You open the windows, doors, and cabinets to let good luck flow into the house. Like polka dots in clothes (see previous item), round food items represent coins, and hence encourage the coming of wealth in the year ahead.

Some Koreans believe that if you cut your toenails after dark, the discarded cuttings can form a spirit which can hurt you.

In Korea some drinkers think it's bad luck to order bottles of beer in even numbers. So if two Koreans are drinking, they'll often order three beers. In some small rural towns it's hard to find six-packs or cases of 12 beers for the same reason. On your birthday it is lucky to have three parties, with three different groups of people in three different places. Usually you'll have one at home, then one out and then another at another home.

In Burma children are taught never to awaken anyone too abruptly, in case their wandering soul does not have time to return to the body—in which case, they will die immediately.

General

If you blow out all the candles on your birthday cake with the first puff you will get your wish.

Among the superstitions connected with singing is one enshrined in this rhyme:

> "Sing before seven, Cry before eleven."

Seeing an ambulance is very unlucky unless you pinch your nose or hold your breath until you see a black or a brown dog.

To avoid catching a cold during the winter, you need to ensure you catch a falling leaf on the first day of fall.

To be forced to call in a doctor on a Friday was a very bad omen for the patient's recovery.

The first patient to be treated in a doctor's new office, or a new hospital, is certain to be cured.

The best doctor is the seventh child of a seventh child.

It was once thought bad luck to pay a physician's bill in full: it implied an excessive confidence in the return of full health.

Among the many ways of passing on bodily misfortune to others is the following way of curing a sty in the eye: stand at a crossroads and chant:

> "Sty, sty, leave my eye,
> Take the next one coming by."

Your sty will be transfer itself to the (unfortunate) passer-by who is the next person to happen along the crossroads.

Children's common terror of stepping on a crack in the sidewalk finds expression in a sinister old rhyme:

> "Step on a crack
> Break your mother's back."

The sound of bells drives away demons because they're afraid of the loud noise and when a bell rings, a new angel has received his wings.

The opal is reputed to be unlucky to all except those were born in October. It is particularly bas luck to have an opal engagement ring.

Shoes can be a potent source of bad luck. Never leave them upside-down, and never put them on the table, for this will cause bad luck for the rest of the day.

It used to be said that "a whistling girl rouses the devil." This belief grew from general attitudes concerning the proper station of women in society. It was also proverbial that "a whistling woman and a crowing hen are neither fit for God nor men." A crowing (as opposed to merely clucking) hen was clearly usurping the prerogatives of the rooster. A hen that sported tail-feathers like those of a rooster was also being presumptuous. All these were regarded as portents of bad luck.

Parents and teachers still sometimes tell their charges that "a blister will rise upon one's tongue that tells a lie."

The Blarney Stone is a stone set in the wall of the tower of Blarney Castle in the Irish village of Blarney. Kissing the stone, while hanging upside down, is supposed to bring the kisser the gift of persuasive eloquence ("blarney").

If you say good-bye to a friend on a bridge, you will never see each other again.

If you lean a broom against a bed, it will cast an evil spell on the bed and bring bad luck to those who sleep in it.

If you sweep over an unmarried person's feet, they'll never get married.

Don't take an old broom into a new house—it's bad luck. Get a new broom.

If you sweep an unwelcome guest's room as soon as they have departed, they won't return.

If a candle lighted as part of a ceremony blows out, it is a sign that evil spirits are nearby.

If you get gooseflesh (goosebumps) or a chill up your back, it means that someone is walking over your grave.

Evil spirits can't harm you when you stand inside a circle.

It's bad luck to leave a house through a door other than the one you came in by.

It is unlucky to let a flag touch the ground.

Be sure to hang that horseshoe the right way up (with the two ends pointing upward); the luck will "run out" if you place it the wrong way round.

The hopeful belief has arisen among scholars that if you use the same pencil when taking an examination that you used when studying for the test, the pencil will remember—and write—the answers.

If someone rises from a rocking-chair and leaves it rocking, evil spirits are liable to enter the house in order to enjoy sitting in it.

Finding a pair of gloves is an omen that a new love relationship is about to begin—perhaps even a marriage.

Someone who drinks too much can be cured by placing a live eel in their drink.

Spitting on the hands when starting to dig is not just a matter of protecting the hands against blistering: it is a magic spell to give oneself more strength for the task.

Sports players should spit on a new bat before using it for the first time to make it lucky.

In Ireland it was thought that the father of new baby should spit on the child to bring it luck.

If a clock which has not been working suddenly chimes, there will be a death in the family.

Whenever there is a lull in conversation, someone is likely to announce that an angel is passing. It is said to happen especially at 20 minutes before or after the hour.

Coral charms are still widely believed to protect their wearer from evil spells and natural disasters such as lightning or bad winds. They were traditionally hung about the necks of children and babies. The color of the coral is said to indicate the wearer's state of health: it grows pale as the person grows more ill and recovers its color as he regains his health.

Proverbs

So many proverbs have seeped into our everyday language that when you scan a collection of them, they seem more like common parlance than wise old sayings. In the next section, there are gathered together some of the most bizarre, obscure, politically incorrect, and fascinating proverbs from around the world. Some of them show a typical national characteristic, some are laughably chauvinistic, and some just deal with the care of goats.

On the basis that it's better not to sit down and explain jokes, there has been no serious attempt to dissect every proverb contained in this collection and give the underlying truism. Some of them defy analysis.

Scandinavia

NORWAY

You don't have to put out the fire when all is burnt out.

Climbing the fence at its lowest point is not shame if you have to.

The headless army can be in for a hard time.

The summer moments always pass quickly.

Exposing yourself to danger, by weapons in hand, is bad.

There is no shame in clothing you have not cut yourself.

It's bad to get ashamed over a thing well grasped.

Poor thanks is the way of the world.

When the glacier sees the spring sun, it weeps.

Who marries in too great haste ends up as a half-slave at his place.

It's no shame to look into the warm spring sun and regret a lost limb.

A weeping suitor, a barefoot smith, a runaway horse, and a stammering minister—who do you prefer?

Anyone has to live on top of good customs where he is settled.

In every woman there is a Queen. Speak to the Queen and the Queen will answer.

On the road between the homes of friends, grass does not grow.

If the glacier perceives a headless army is clumsy, it feels a kind of emphatic guilt.

The lame man runs if he has to.

Heroism consists of hanging on one minute longer.

It is better to feed one cat than many mice.

You will not choke on big words and bacon fat.

FINLAND

On the gallows, the first night is the worst.

Life is uncertain so eat your dessert first.

There's a man who looks like a partridge with legs like a mosquito.

War does not determine who is right, only who is remaining.

Cows' diets have never been sustained on grass grown in May.

Work doesn't scare him, but he could lay down near it and sleep.

Love came in a paper bag, said the maiden when she got a letter from her sweetheart.

Swamp there, water here, not dry anywhere.

A man comes back from beyond the seas, not from under the sod.

Time for the mouse to yawn when it's half inside the cat.

A fool boasts of his horse, a madman of his wife, the skilless his children.

Don't go to the sauna if you're not itching.

A bit of dirt adds to the soup, a spider to the dough.

The box chooses its lid.

It shrinks like a partridge before the end of the world.

Laughter from long joy, a fart from laughing long.

Poverty is no joy, although it sometimes makes you laugh.

The frost drives the pig home.

No need to plough and sow madmen, they grow by themselves.

He stares like a cow at a new gate.

Don't mistake the bone for meat, nor a sheep's head for a roasted turnip.

Even the crow sings with its own voice.

There will always be branch grabbers, while there are fir-tree haulers.

If tar, hard liquor, and the sauna do not cure; the disease is fatal.

A snotnose may grow up to be a man; but he who laughs without cause, never.

The forest will answer you in the way you call to it.

SWEDEN

A piece of bread in the pocket is worth more than a feather in the hat.

Don't throw away the old bucket until you're sure the new one holds water.

The afternoon knows what the morning never suspected.

Advice should be viewed from behind.

Fear less, hope more, eat less, chew more, whine less, breathe more, talk less, say more, hate less, love more, and all good things will be yours.

Love is like dew that falls on both nettles and lilies.

The best place to find a helping hand is at the end of your own arm.

Thou shalt not muzzle the ox that treadeth out the corn.

What can you expect from a pig but a grunt?

Don't let your sorrow come higher than your knees.

In the shallowest waters, the ugliest fish swim.

You should not paint the devil on the wall.

When you're speaking about the trolls, they're standing in the entrance hall.

Evil gun powder doesn't go away easily.

Lick upward, kick downward.

"Sour" said the fox about rowanberries.

Don't sell the fur until the bear has been shot.

Even the sun has got spots.

If a blind man leads another, they both fall down together.

Those who wish to sing, always find a song.

DENMARK

Food tastes best when you eat it with your own spoon.

Judge a maiden at the kneading trough, not at the dance.

What you cannot say briefly you do not know.

After three days, both fish and guests begin to smell.

God gives every bird its food but does not drop it into the nest.

Never sail out further than you can row back.

A bad haircut is two people's shame.

A bird never flew on one wing.

A cow is not called dappled unless she has a spot.

A crow is never the whiter for often washing.

A duck will not always dabble in the same gutter.

A foul mouth must be provided with a strong back.

A green Christmas makes a fat churchyard.

A gross belly does not produce a refined mind.

A head is not to be cut off because it is scabby.

A little dog, a cow without horns, and a short man, are generally proud.

A man does not look behind the door unless he has stood there himself.

A man must keep his mouth open a long while before a roast pigeon files into it.

A man's character reaches town before his person.

A stepmother has a hard hand.

A woman may be ever so old, but if you set her on fire, she will jump.

Act in the valley so that you need not fear those who stand on the hill.

Advice after the mischief is like medicine after death.

After pleasant scratching comes unpleasant smarting.

All who snore are not asleep.

An honest man is not the worse because a dog barks at him.

An ill-tempered woman is the devil's doornail.

Better a salt herring on your own table, than a fresh pike on another man's.

Better make a short circuit than to wet your hose.

Bite not the dog that bites.

He does not live in this world that can skin a grindstone.

He is little suited to be a baker, whose head is made of butter.

He must have clean fingers who would blow another's nose.

Children and drunken men speak the truth.

Dull scissors make crooked-mouthed tailors.

Even clever hens sometimes lay their eggs among nettles.

Every bird needs its own feathers.

Every little fish expects to become a whale.

Everything has an end—except a sausage, which has two.

Few women turn gray because their husband dies.

For a good dinner and a gentle wife, you can afford to wait.

From clogs to clogs is only three generations.

Give to a pig when it grunts, and a child when it cries, and you will have a fine pig, and a bad child.

Gray hairs are death's blossoms.

Hang the young thief, and the old one will not steal.

He that touches pitch defiles himself.

He that was born under a three-halfpenny planet shall never be worth twopence

He who can sit upon a stone and feed himself should not move.

He who has a white horse and a fair wife is seldom without trouble.

He who has no falcon, must hunt with owls.

He who herds with wolves, learns to howl.

A man who sows peas on the highway does not get all the pods into his barn.

He who tastes every man's broth, often burns his mouth.

He who was born to be hanged will not be drowned, unless the water go over the gallows.

Lawyers and painters can soon change white to black.

Many a cow stands in the meadow and looks wistfully at the common.

No and yes cause long disputes.

No one can be caught in places he does not visit.

He who would buy sausage of a dog must give him bacon in exchange.

He who would drive another over three dikes must climb over two himself.

Help is good everywhere, except in the porridge bowl.

In still water the worms are worst.

It is a bold mouse that makes her nest in the cat's ear.

It is bad for puppies to play with bear cubs.

It is easy to poke another man's fire.

It is not easy to sting a bear with a straw.

It is not every hog that the crow will ride.

It is vain to fish without a hook, or learn to read without a book.

One knows what the dinner was after the plates have been washed.

One would rather be bitten by wolves than by sheep.

Praise is not pudding.

Money is more eloquent than a dozen members of parliament.

Praise the child, and you make love to the mother.

Sparrows should not dance with cranes, their legs are too short.

Take advice of a red-bearded man, and be gone.

The best manure is under the farmer's shoe.

The dog's kennel is not the place to keep a sausage.

The owl thinks her children are the fairest.

They who do not wash well, do not bleach well.

To cut into another's man's ear is like cutting into a felt hat.

"We are all well-placed," said the cat, when she was seated on the bacon.

When neighbors quarrel, lookers-on are more apt to add fuel than water.

When the rooks are silent the swans begin to sing.

When the wolf's ears appear, his body is not far off.

You cannot drink and whistle at the same time.

You must walk a long while behind a wild goose before you find an ostrich feather.

A flying crow always catches something.

ICELAND

Mediocrity is climbing molehills without sweating,

Eastern Europe

RUSSIA

Every seed knows its time.

Any fish is good if it is on the hook.

An onion treats seven ailments.

Better a dove on the plate than a woodgrouse in the mating place.

You cannot break through a wall with your forehead.

There will be trouble if the cobbler starts making pies.

Any sandpiper is great in his own swamp.

Not everyone who has a cowl on is a monk.

Do not carry rubbish out of your hut.

One does not go to Tula with one's own samovar.

Chickens are counted in the autumn.

Do not measure (others) by your own arshin.

Do not teach a pike to swim, a pike knows his own science.

One is one's own master on one's own stove.

A good merchant has neither money nor goods.

A priest's belly is made up of several sheepskins.

Don't drive a binya into the woods if he has found his way to your house.

Not everything is a mermaid that dives into the water.

Old age is not a joy, but death is not a gain.

Peace lasts till the army comes, and the army lasts till peace comes.

The horse loves oats; the earth, manure; and the governor.

A cat always knows whose meat it eats.

A guest has not to thank the host, but the host the guest.

A mile walk with a friend has only one hundred steps.

A word of kindness is better than a fat pie.

If the pocket is empty, the judge is deaf.

Tell God the truth, but give the judge money.

Long whiskers cannot take the place of brains.

Confide a secret to a dumb man and he will speak.

Deprive a mirror of its silver and even The Tsar won't see his face.

Don't put it in my ear, but in my hand.

Even a blind pig finds an acorn every once in awhile.

Fear the goat from the front, the horse from the rear, and man from all sides.

God wanted to chastise mankind, so he sent lawyers.

Having a good wife and rich cabbage soup, seek not other things.

Love and eggs are best when they are fresh.

Until you have smoked out the bees, you can't eat the honey.

Pray to God but continue to row to the shore.

Success has many fathers, while failure is an orphan.

The fall of a leaf is a whisper to the living.

The first cup of vodka goes as a stake, the second as a falcon, and the third as a little bird.

The rich would have to eat money if the poor did not provide food.

The tallest blade of grass is the first to be cut by the scythe.

The tongue always returns to the sore tooth.

It's a hard winter when one wolf eats another.

Vodka is the aunt of wine.

You do not really understand something unless you can explain it to your grandmother.

The wolf will hire himself out very cheaply as a shepherd.

Devils live in quiet pond.

Wild ducks and tomorrow, both come without calling.

A field held in common is always ravaged by bears.

A jug that has been mended lasts two hundred years.

An icy May fills the granaries.

Bad luck is fertile.

Don't worry if you borrow, but worry if you lend.

If you put your nose into water, you will also wet your cheeks.

One son is no son, two sons is no son, but three sons is a son.

Sit a beggar at your table and he will soon put his feet on it.

The horses of hope gallop, but the asses of experience go slowly.

The coat is quite new, only the holes are old.

When roubles falls from heaven there is no sack, when there is a sack roubles don't fall from heaven.

When you live next to the cemetery you cannot weep for everyone.

It is easier for the horse, when a woman is off the cart.

Every vegetable has its time.

Only the brave will change the hunchback.

If you feel the need to work, take a nap, the need will pass.

You can't spoil porridge with butter.

Your tongue can get you to Kiev.

HUNGARY

A prudent man does not make the goat his gardener.

A puff of wind and popular praise weigh the same.

Whoever gets mixed up with bran will be eaten by pigs.

Every miracle lasts only three days.

He whose place is on the gallows, will not die in the Danube.

The truth is that there are no witches.

He who cannot speak Arabic, should not speak Arabic.

Believe in women as in the weather in April.

Even an owl is a judge in its own cave.

The owl tells the sparrow that her head is big.

Tell me who your friend is, and I'll tell you who you are.

It is below the bottom of a frog.
(It is of inferior quality.)

Former highwaymen make the best policemen.

Like Mrs Bodó he talks about something **else** when asked to pay for the wine.

A fool stumbles twice at the same stone.

A fool may throw a stone into a well which a hundred wise men cannot take out.

Pepper is small but strong.

Every one carries his own skin to the market.

He is one pamphlet behind the others.

The castle of Buda was not built in one day.

There was a dog market in Buda only once.

I would not wipe my muddy boots on him.

He keeps silent, like a deaf pig in the wheat field.

Do not waste your ginger on pigs.

Many geese overpower a pig.

Two dogs never agree on one bone.

You do not need a basket to pick well-known strawberries.
(*Because someone will already have got there first.*)

Running away is a shame, but it is useful.

It was needed as a Slovak glazier needed falling on his back.
(Or...*I needed that like a hole in the head.*)

Postpone today's anger till tomorrow.

Many homes burn inside but it is not seen outside.

Do not trust even your own shirt.

Having no ointment and box why do you pose as hairdresser?

Tastes and slaps are different.

He can live even on flat ice.

A kiss without a beard is like an egg without salt.

Even an old goat likes to lick salt.

Even old men like making love.

He drinks like a brushmaker. (*Like a fish.*)

We shall write the debt in soot on the chimney.
(*We may as well write it off straight away.*)

He shouts snake and frog at somebody.
(*To abuse somebody.*)

Long sausage and short sermons are good.

It is an egg of Columbus.
(*It's a very easy problem to solve.*)

One blacksmith envies another.

You may go to Kukutyin to sharpen oats.
(*You're not needed any more.*)

A red (haired) dog, a red (haired) horse, a red (haired) man—none of them are good.

The horse should worry, he has a big head.

He goes around it like a cat goes around hot mush.

They grind in two mills.
(*They speak of different things.*)

He that is not a master of something, is a butcher of it.

He who is sitting in the reeds, makes a whistle of his choice.

There are more days than sausages.

An arrow once shot is hard to get back.

An ox remains an ox even if driven to Vienna.

He may go to the salt office.
(*His case will not be heard anywhere.*)

He will disappear like a gray donkey in the fog.

Do not stir the manure if you do not want the smell to get even worse.

Sing the song of the man whose cart you sit on.

He knows as much about it as a hen does about the alphabet.

It is not good to eat cherries from the same dish with persons of high rank.

He who has butter on his head, should not go in the sun.

Against a thousand crows, one stone is enough.

He could not earn enough to buy even cold water.

CZECH REPUBLIC

The big thieves hang the little ones.

He who cannot cut the bread evenly cannot get on well with people.

The discontented child cries for toasted snow.

It is better to have your house burn down twice rather than move once. (*!*)

Hint to the smart, but kick the stupid one.

He who doesn't steal, steals from his family.

He who is (too) curious shall grow old soon.

Better a sparrow in the hand than a pigeon on the roof.

A lie has short legs.

Many a friend was lost through a joke, but none was ever gained so.

Czech beer makes beautiful bodies.

A hundred bakers, a hundred millers, and a hundred tailors are three hundred thieves.

Western Europe

GERMANY

A country can be judged by the quality of its proverbs.

A blind man swallows many flies.

A fence lasts three years, a dog lasts three fences, a horse three dogs, and a man three horses.

A handful of might is better than a sackful of right.

A swindler who cannot pass off mouse-turd for pepper, has not learned his trade.

A lawyer and the wheel of the cart must be greased.

A pack of cards is the devil's prayer book.

A young doctor means a new graveyard.

All skill is in vain when an angel pees in the touch-hole of your musket.

Affectation is a greater injury to the face than smallpox.

An old man loved is a winter with flowers.

April weather, woman's love, rose-leaves, dice, and card-luck, change every moment.

Asses sing badly, because they pitch their voices too high.

Better, "There he goes," than, "There he hangs."

Cheese and bread make the cheeks red.

Bargains are costly.

Coffee and love are best when they are hot.

Do not ship all in one bottom.

Either fight not with priests or beat them to death.(*!*)

Every cock crows best on his own dunghill.

FRANCE

With a young hunter, one needs an old dog.

No one knows better than the ass where the pack wounds it.

Corn grows well in a small field.

Insane and simple is the ewe that makes the wolf his confessor.

It is better to lose a witty remark than a friend.

A muzzled cat never took mice.

Eagles don't breed doves.

Love and poverty do bad housework together.

L'art est de cacher l'art. Or... Art is to hide art.

A woman's advice is no great thing, but he who won't take it is a fool.

The hunchback does not see his hump, but sees that of his fellow man.

The money hammer will open the iron door.

One does not go to the mill with the beauty of one's wife.

A cow does not know what her tail is worth until she has lost it.

A crooked log makes a good fire.

A fence between, makes love more keen.

A fine girl and a tattered gown always find something to hook them.

A full belly sets a man jigging.

Who eats chicken, chicken comes to him.

The eye of the master does more than both his hands.

An old rat easily finds a hole.

A spider in the morning, anguish; a spider in the evening, hope.

With ifs, one could put Paris in a bottle.

A big nose never spoiled a handsome face.

A clown enriched knows neither relation nor friend.

A crooked stick will have a crooked shadow.

A deaf husband and a blind wife are always a happy couple.

A father is a banker provided by nature.

A fool's heart dances on his lips.

A glaring sunny morning, a woman that talks Latin, and a child reared on wine, never come to a good end.

A good fox does not eat his neighbor's fowls.

A good head does not want for hats.

A great fortune in the hands of a fool is a great misfortune.

A handful of good life is better than seven barrels of learning.

A hungry dog will eat dirty pudding.

A lame man won't walk with one who is lamer.

A little sheep always seems young.

A man at sixteen will prove a child at sixty.

A man who is his own lawyer has a fool for a client.

A man with a watch knows what time it is. A man with two watches is never sure.

A person is unlucky who falls on his back and breaks his nose.

A pig's life, short and sweet.

A sow is always dreaming of bran.

A woman and a melon are hard to choose.

A woman and a ship ever want mending.

A woman's tongue is her sword, and she does not let it rust.

An old ape never made a pretty grimace.

Every potter vaunts his own pot.

God saves the moon from the wolves.

Happy is the man who has a handsome wife close to an abbey.

He is a horse with four white feet (*i.e. unlucky*).

He is a very bad manager of honey who leaves nothing to lick off his fingers.

He is like a singed cat, better than he looks.

Avarice bursts the bag.

Better a good dinner than a fine coat.

Better be an old man's darling than a young man's slave.

Better to wear out than rust out.

By candlelight a goat looks like a lady.

Do not lend your money to a great man.

Don't snap your fingers at the dogs before you are out of the village.

Don't talk Latin before the Franciscans.

Empty rooms make giddy housewives.

Every fool likes his bauble.

Every one takes a flogging in his own way.

Do not strip before bedtime.

He is like the gardener's dog, who doesn't eat cabbages and will let no one else eat them.

He lies like a toothdrawer.

He puts his sickle into another man's harvest.

Never put your finger between the tree and the bark.

No man is an island, but some of us are long peninsulas.

No one with a good catch of fish goes home by the back alley.

Nothing so bold as a miller's shirt (*because it takes a thief by the throat every morning*).

He that telleth his wife news is but lately married.

He that that hath a head of wax must not approach the fire.

He that would go to sea for pleasure would go to hell for a pastime.

He who never budges from Paris will never be pope.

He who sees leather cut asks for a thong.

He will not lose his oats for want of braying

In the end it will be known who ate the bacon.

It is a stupid goose that listens to the fox preach.

It is a sorry house in which the cock is silent and the hen crows.

It is good to beat a proud man when he is alone.

Let not your shirt know your way of thinking.

Love Bertrand, love his dog.

One always knocks oneself in the sore place.

One blind man leads another into the ditch.

One may steal nothing except a lawyer's purse.

A man should choose a wife with his ears, rather than with his eyes.

The best company must part, as King Dagobert said to his hounds.

The devil was so fond of his children that he plucked out their eyes.

The Emperor of Germany is the king of kings; the King of Spain, king of men; the King of France, king of asses; the King of England, king of devils.

The fox says of the mulberries, when he cannot get at them; they are not good at all.

A fox thinks that everybody eats poultry like himself.

The Germans carry their wit in their fingers.

The greatest king must at last go to bed with a shovel.
(*i.e. when he's dead and buried*)

The hen ought not to cackle in the presence of the cock.

The miser and the pig are of no use till they are both dead.

War is much too serious a matter to be left in the hands of the military.

When all you have is a hammer, everything looks like a nail.

The mountaineer's ass carries wine and drinks water.

There is no spite so great as that of a proud beggar.

There is no such thing as a pretty good omelette

There's no need to grease the fat pig's rump.

There never was a mirror that told a woman she was ugly.

When the Frenchman sleeps, the devil rocks him.

Think much, say little, write less.

To a good cat, a good rat.

To grow rich one has only to turn his back on God.

To rob a robber is not robbing.

To wash an ass's head is but loss of time and soap.
(*To reprove a fool is a waste of time and energy.*)

Trust not to God but upon good locks.

Two men may meet, but never two mountains.

Vanity has no greater foe than vanity.

Where the hostess is pretty, the wine is good.

Where the wine is good, the hostess is pretty.

Write injuries in the sand and kindnesses in marble.

The old monkey gets the apple.

The reputation of a man is like his shadow; it sometimes follows and sometimes precedes him. It is sometimes longer and sometimes shorter than his natural size.

The worst clothed go to windward.

IRELAND

A Tyrone woman will never buy a rabbit without a head for fear its a cat.

Soft words butter no parsnips but they won't harden the heart of the cabbage either.

Marriages are all happy, its having breakfast together that causes all the trouble.

What butter and whiskey will not cure there's no cure for.

Drink is the curse of the land. It makes you fight with your neighbor. It makes you shoot at your landlord and it makes you miss him.

Firelight will not let you read fine stories but it's warm and you won't see the dust on the floor.

Many an Irish property was increased by the lace of a daughter's petticoat.

Even a tin knocker will shine on a dirty door.

An old broom knows the dirty corners best.

Any man can lose his hat in a fairy-wind.

It's as hard to see a woman crying as it is to see a barefooted duck.

It's a bad hen that won't scratch herself.

Snuff at a wake is fine if there's nobody sneezing over the snuff box.

A silent mouth is melodious.

A blind man can see his mouth.

A live dog is better than a dead lion.

Put a beggar on horseback and he'll ride to hell.

The hole is more honorable than the patch.

Poor men take to the sea; the rich to the mountains.

It is no time to go for the doctor when the patient is dead.

Men are like bagpipes, no sound comes from them until they're full.

It's better to return from the center of the ford than drown in the flood.

The horse with the most scars is the one that kicks his rear highest.

The person who brings a story to you will take two away from you.

A greyhound finds food in its feet.

Fences have ears.

Don't tell your secret even to a fence.

Woe to the man that entrusts his secrets to a ditch.

It's bad manners to talk about ropes in the house of a man whose father was hanged.

He couldn't drag a herring off the coals.

The doorstep of a great house is slippery.

There's little value in the single cow.

Going in is not the same as going out.

He may die of wind but he'll never die of wisdom.

Irishwomen have a dispensation from the pope to wear the thick ends of their legs downwards.

A whistling woman and a crowing hen will bring no luck to the house they are in.

The poor lack much, but the greedy more.

I'll go there tonight for evening is speedier than morning.

Nature breaks out through the eyes of the cat.

The lake is no heavier for the duck which is on it.

Listen to the sound of the river and you will get a trout.

Hunger is a good sauce.

When the stomach is full, the bones like to stretch.

The drunkard takes the roof from his own house and puts it on the publican's house.

Beware of the drinking house or you'll be living on barnacles.

Peace is better than a hundred cows on a hill.

He has eaten the calf in the cow's stomach.
(*He has gone into debt on the assumption that he can clear it in the future.*)

The person who would give you a story would take two stories away from you.

If it is not dry, it is better wet.

It won't always be raining.

Get your wife locally, but far from you sell your cow.

If you only have a male goat, be in the middle of the fair with it.

It is hard to whistle and eat at the same time.

One bite of a rabbit is better than two bites of a cat.

Little things tend to be tasty.

Don't keep your tongue under your belt.

The one who opens his mouth the most, 'tis he who opens his purse the least.

An empty sack does not stand.

A man takes a drink, the drink takes a drink, the drink takes the man.

Never bolt your door with a boiled carrot.

If it's drowning you're after, don't torment yourself with shallow water.

The pig in the sty doesn't know the pig going along the road.

Seeing is believing, but feeling is God's own truth.

You must take the little potato with the big potato.

You've got to do your own growing, no matter how tall your grandfather was.

When one shuts one eye, one does not hear everything.

It's no use boiling your cabbage twice.

A boy's best friend is his mother, and there's no tie stronger than her apron string.

A live dog is better than a dead lion.

The old pipe gives the sweetest smoke.

One pair of good soles is better than two pairs of good uppers.

If you lie down with dogs, you'll get up with fleas.

A goat in a silk dress is still a goat.

In winter, the milk goes to the cow's horns.

It's no use carrying an umbrella if your shoes are leaking.

It's hard to choose between two blind goats.

ENGLAND

A goose quill is more dangerous than a lion's claw.
(*The pen is mightier than the sword etc.*)

A leap year is never a good sheep year.

Big boast, small roast.

Children suck the mother when they are young and the father when they are old.

Do when ye may, or suffer ye the nay, in love 'tis the way.

In a cat's eye, all things belong to cats.

Raw cucumber makes the churchyards prosperous.

Spring has come when you can put your foot on three daisies.

A fair October and a good blast, will blow the hag and her broom away fast.

Autumn steals summer like a thief.

Every mile in winter is two.

He that takes the devil into his boat must carry him over the sound.

A lie well stuck to is as good as the truth.

Scratch an Englishman, and you'll find a seaman

Servants, like ornaments, should be kept in their proper places.

There are a thousand hacking at the branches of evil, to one who is striking at the root.

When a cow tries to scratch its ear, it means a shower be very near. When it begins to thump its rib with its tail, look out for thunder, lightning, and hail.
(*But check the weather forecast anyway.*)

SCOTLAND

Never let your feet run faster than your shoes.

The devil's boots don't creak.

They that smell least, smell best.

Willful waste makes woeful want.

A deaf man will hear the clink o' money.

Whaur there's a Jock there's a Jenny.

Choose yer wife wi' her nichtcap on.

Them that herd swine always hear them gruntin'.

A scabbit sheep will smit the hale hirsel'.

Bitin' and scartin' are Scots fowks wooin.

As auld as the Moss o' Meigle.

A guid tale is no' the waur o' bein' twice tauld.

Everything has an end and a pudden has twa.

There's nane sae blind as them that winna see.

Marry yer son when ye will, but yer dochter when ye can.

Money's like the muck midden, it deas nae guid till it be spreed.

Mebbie's a big wurd.

A bark frae a toothless dug is as guid as a bite.

A midgie's as big as a mountain... amaist.

A silverless man gangs fast throu the mercat.

Muckledom is nae virtue.

Pigs micht whistle, but they hae a ill mooth for't.

Pride that dines wi' vanity sups wi' contempt.

Poets an painters is aye puir.

A daft nurse maks a wise wean.

A fidging mare should be wed girded.

Scotsmen aye taks their mark frae a mischief.

Self praise comes aye stinkin' ben.

Shame's past the shed o' yer hair.

Smaa fish is better than nane.

She leuks like butter wouldna melt in her mou'.

Sodgers, fire, an watter suin mak room for theirsel's.

As the fool thinks the bell clinks.

Give a man luck and fling him in the sea.

Speak guid o pipers, yer faither wis a fiddler.

SPAIN

For lack of good men, they made my father mayor.

To a skinny dog, all are fleas.

Raise a raven, and it will peck out your eyes.

When the indian slides on his backside, there's no way to stop him.

It's better to arrive at the right moment than to be invited.

If your wife wants to throw you off the roof, try to find a low one.

Never advise anyone to go to war or to marry.

Books are hindrances to persisting stupidity.

It's not the same to talk of bulls as to be in the bullring.

A pig bought on credit is forever grunting.

An ounce of mother is worth a pound of clergy.

A rich man is either a scoundrel or the heir of a scoundrel.

Blessed is he who expects nothing, for he shall never be disappointed.

Better have a bad ass than be your own ass.

The hole invites the thief.

A mistress in a high place is not a bad thing.

A dog does not always bark at the front gate.

Better a quiet death than a public misfortune.

God gives almonds to those who have no teeth.

Halfway is twelve miles when you have fourteen miles to go.

He that has a good harvest must put up with a few thistles.

He that marries a widow will often have a dead man's head thrown into the dish.

If the sky falls, hold up your hands.

If you want good service, serve yourself.

It is better to conceal one's knowledge than to reveal one's ignorance.

Let your heart guide your head in evil matters.

Love is like war; begin when you like and leave off when you can.

The best mirror is an old friend.

The fear of women is the basis of good health.

Visit your aunt, but not every day of the year.

ITALY

A cat that licks the spit is not to be trusted with roast meat.
(*Which begs the question, how many cats would you trust with the roast meat in the first place?*)

A drowning man would clutch at razors.

A new broom is good for three days.

A loud cry but little wool, as the man said who shaved the sow.

He who goes to the mill gets befloured.

He who has a straw tail is always afraid of it catching fire.

He who has money to throw away, let him employ workmen, and not stand by.

Greater fools than they of Zago, who put dung on the steeple to make it grow.

A threatened buffet is never well given.

A woman who loves to be at the window is like a bunch of grapes on the wayside.

An ass's tail will not make a sieve.

At last the foxes all meet at the furrier's.

Below the navel there is neither religion nor truth.

Boil stones in butter, and you may sip the broth.

Curses are like processions, they return to where they set out.

Does your neighbor love you? Lend him a sequin.

Eggs have no business dancing with stones.

Even a frog would bite if it had teeth.

Every dog is allowed one bite.

He is in search of a ram with five feet.

He who eats pears with his master should not choose the best.

Every potter praises his pot, and most of all the one that is cracked.

Every time history repeats itself the price goes up.

Friends tie their purses with a spider's web.

Glowworms are not lanterns.

God save me from him who has but one occupation.

God save you from a bad neighbor, and from a beginner on the fiddle.

He has done like the Perugian who, when his head was broken, ran home for his helmet.

He hangs the May-branch at every door.
(*Following the Italian custom of young men hanging out May branches overnight in front of the door of their lover.*)

He who is an ass and thinks himself a stag, finds his mistake when he comes to leap the ditch.

He who lets the goat be laid on his shoulders is soon after forced to carry the cow. He who wants milk should not sit in the middle of a field and wait for a cow to back up to him.

It is not spring until you can plant your foot upon twelve daisies.

Many return from the war who cannot give an account of the battle.

No sooner is the law made than its evasion is discovered.

Never let the sun go down on your anger.

No sooner is the law made than its evasion is discovered.

Australasia

ABORIGINAL

Those who play at bowls must look out for rubbers.

Those who lose dreaming are lost.

MAORI

The brave man who climbs trees is food for their roots.

Persist in all things as resolutely as you persist in eating.

TAHITI

Water only flows into rivers.

(*Money goes only to the wealthy.*)

Africa

AFRICAN PROVERBS

A bird does not change its feathers because the weather is bad.

A fool looks for dung where the cow never browsed.

A man who has one finger pointing at another has three pointing toward himself.

A man who is trampled to death by an elephant must have been blind and deaf.

A masked performer who tries too hard to outclass his colleagues may expose his backside.

A sick person cannot survive if a greedy eater is allowed nearby.

An oil lamp feels proud to give light, even though it uses itself up.

Do not call to a dog with a whip in your hand.

Do not look where you fell, but where you slipped.

Do not speak of a rhinoceros if there is no tree nearby.

Do not tell the man who is carrying you that he stinks.

Does a man not know when he has pepper in his eyes?

Every river knows the places where the earth will not soak up its water—and that is where it flows.

He who is afraid of doing too much always does too little.

He who is being carried does not realize how far the town is.

If one person in a street kills a dog, the street is called a street of dog-killers.

If there were no elephant in the jungle, the buffalo would be a great animal.

If things are getting easier, maybe you're going downhill.

If you run after two hares you will catch neither.

Indecision is like a stepchild: if he does not wash his hands, he is called dirty; if he does, he is told he is wasting water.

It is not only the hyena—even the snail arrives at its destination.

It is the calm and silent water that drowns a man.

It is the toothless animal that arrives first at the base of the fruit tree, to eat its fill before others arrive.

It is when there is a stampede that the person with big buttocks becomes conscious of his load.

No one tests the depth of the river with both feet.

One camel does not make fun of another camel's hump.

The end of an ox is beef, and the end of a lie is grief.

The fly that has no one to advise it follows the corpse into the grave.

The fowl perspires, but the feathers do not allow us to see the perspiration.

The frog wanted to be as big as the elephant, and burst.

The goat that cries the loudest is not the one that will eat the most.

The leech that does not let go, even when it is filled, dies on the dry land.

When a fool is cursed, he thinks he is being praised.

When a fowl gets to a new town, it stands on one leg until it learns that it is a place where people stand on two legs.

When a man's coat is threadbare, it is easy to pick a hole in it.

When a ripe fruit sees an honest man, it drops.

When a woman prepares a dish which others dislike, she claims that she prepared it to suit her own taste.

When elephants fight, it is the grass that suffers.

When spiders unite, they can tie down a lion.

When the bee comes to your house, let her have beer; you may wish to visit her house some day.

When the master is absent, the frogs hop into the house.

Whether the knife falls on the melon or the melon on the knife, it is the melon that suffers.

You cannot build a house for last year's summer.

You can't go back to the farmer who gave you seed yams to plant to complain that beetles have eaten them up.

MOROCCO

An old cat will not learn how to dance.

Either do as your neighbors do, or move away.

If you are a peg, endure the knocking; if you are a mallet, strike.

The pumpkin gives birth and the fence has the trouble.

The tar of my country is better than the honey of others.

Work and you will be strong; sit and you will stink.

MADAGASCAR

A canoe does not know who is king. When it turns over, everyone gets wet.

A patient who can swallow food makes the nurse doubtful.

An egg does not fight a rock.

Cross in a crowd and the crocodile won't eat you.

Crows bewail the dead sheep, and then eat them.

Disgraced—like a man whose own pet bites him.

Do not be like a miser who saves for those who will bury him.

Do not treat your loved one like the swinging door that you are fond of but push back and forth.

Like roosters' tail feathers: pretty but always behind.

Sorrow is like rice in an attic: you use a little every day and at the end it is all gone.

The lazy man who goes to borrow a spade says, "I hope I will not find one."

SWAHILI

Help comes in two ways, death or healing.

There is no season of heavy rains without mosquitoes.

The fear of God is not wearing a white turban.

Old droppings do not stink.

You may climb a thorn tree, and be unable to come down again.

Running on the roof finishes at the edge.

When a fool becomes enlightened, the wise man is in trouble.

Chill out (*a lot*) like a banana.

When you play with a lion, do not put your hand in its mouth.

A dog with a bone knows no friends.

A donkey's (*re-payment of a*) favor is its fart.

He who laughs at a cripple, has one at home.

One who praises the rain, has been rained upon.

When what is yours rots, you dry it out in the sun (*before it rots some more*).

The sign of rain is clouds.

Don't insult the bridge that you just crossed.

A mango is similar to a banana (*accept what you're given*).

If you can't manage horses; what will you feed the elephants?

A big person with no intellect is a log.

Too many navigators capsize a vessel.

A child's laughter is the roof of a house.

He who chooses (*differentiates between*) spades is not a farmer.

A lion that walks quietly is the one that eats meat

A man who waters his neighbor's cattle must first put his foot in the water hole.

Middle East

ARABIC

A man profits more by the sight of an idiot than by the orations of the learned.

A thousand curses never tore a shirt.

A wise man associating with vice-ridden ones becomes an idiot; a dog traveling with good men grows wise.

All mankind is divided into three classes: those that are immoveable, those that are moveable, and those that move.

An army of sheep led by a lion would defeat an army of lions led by a sheep.

Better a handful of dry dates and contentment than to own the Peacock Gate and be kicked in the eye by a broody camel.

Dawn does not come twice to awaken a man.

Death rides a fast camel.

I am a prince and you are a prince, so who will lead the donkeys?

If I were to trade in winding sheets, no one would die.

If the camel once gets his nose in the tent, the rest of him will follow.

If you buy cheap meat, when it boils you will smell what you have saved.

If you have to be a beggar, make sure you knock only at the largest gates.

If you stop every time a dog barks, your road will never end.

It is good to know the truth, but it is better to talk about palm trees.

Judge a man by the reputation of his enemies.

Let the sword decide after the stratagem has failed.

Live together like brothers and do business like strangers.

Never give advice in a crowd.

On the day of victory no one is tired.

Salt will never be worm-eaten.

Sins of omission are seldom fun.

The moneybox makes more noise when there is one coin in it than when it is full.

The wise man sits on the hole in his carpet.

Throw a lucky man in the sea, and he will come up with a fish in his mouth.

Trust in God, but tie your camel.

AFGHANISTAN

A lame crab walks straight.

A porcupine speaking to its baby says, "O my child of velvet."

Allah has said, "Start moving so that I may start blessing."
(*God helps those who help themselves.*)

Don't show me the palm tree, show me the dates.

Five fingers are brothers but not equals.

Give even an onion graciously.

If you deal in camels, make the doors high.

Only stretch your foot to the length of your blanket.

Storing milk in a sieve, you complain of bad luck?

The mud of one country is the medicine of another.

You can buy twenty-five uncaught sparrows for a penny.

When the tiger kills, the jackal profits.

AZERBAIJAN

I tried to draw the eyebrow, but I ended up poking the eye.

Saying "honey, honey" won't make your mouth sweet.

Until the lions have their historians, tales of the hunt will always glorify the hunter.

EGYPT

Be patient with a bad neighbor: he may move or have some bad luck.

Bed is the poor man's opera.

Making money selling dung is better than losing money selling musk.

Put a rope around your neck and many will be happy to drag you along.

The barking of a dog does not disturb the man on a camel.

KURDISTAN

A cup of coffee may commit one to forty years of friendship.

A neighbor's hen looks as big as a goose, and his wife as young as a girl.

Marriage is a covered dish.
(*You don't know what you're going to get.*)

Every bad has its worse.

If watching could make you skillful, every dog would become a butcher.

It is easier to make a camel jump a ditch than to make a fool listen to reason.

It is easy to catch a serpent with someone else's hand.

Many will show you the way once your cart has overturned.

Of everything else the newest; but of friends, the oldest.

The devil tempts all, but the idle man tempts the devil.

When a cat wants to eat her kittens, she says they look like mice.

PALESTINE

Every sheep is hung by its own leg.

The eye cannot rise above the eyebrow.

PERSIA

A drowning man is not troubled by rain.

A stone thrown at the right time is better than gold given at the wrong time.

An egg thief becomes a camel thief.

SYRIA

Sometimes you have to be silent to be heard.

Good things often come to those who cannot benefit from them.

He hit me—then cried and raced me to complain.

He married the monkey for its money; the money went and the monkey stayed a monkey.

When in doubt who will win, be neutral.

Lacking horses, we saddle the dogs.

Let the water melons break each other!
(*As they do when too many are in one basket; that is, let them stew in their own juice.*)

My brother and I against my cousin, my cousin and I against a stranger.

Never get between a man and his wife.

The camel limped and blamed its split lip.

The child of a duck is a good swimmer

The cock that will be eloquent crows while still in the egg.

Trusting people is like trusting water to remain in a sieve.

When I decided to sell coffins, people decided not to die.

Whoever gets between the onion and its skin will get nothing but its stink.

TURKESTAN

Even if the world is flooded, the duck feels safe.

He gets off his horse but keeps his foot in the stirrup.
(*He wants to hold on to power after resigning from his position.*)

If you can't hit the donkey, hit its saddle.

You can't take back your spit.

Soak the bread with the soup of a flying duck.
(*That is, day-dreaming about something nonexistent.*)

The ear appears first, but the horn grows bigger.

The sky is too high to fly to, the ground is too hard to get into.
(*Accept the circumstances of real life.*)

When the camel's tail touches the ground.
(*When pigs might fly.*)

You may hide the disease, but you won't be able to hide the death.

TURKEY

A single advantage is worth a thousand sorceries.

A thread-bare coat is armor proof against highwaymen.

An ass does not appreciate fruit compote.

An Englishman will burn his bed to catch a flea.

Call the bear "Uncle" till you are safe across the bridge.

Call your husband cuckold in jest and he'll never suspect you.

Even too much praise is a burden.

God postpones, he does not overlook.

Having two ears and one tongue, we should listen twice as much as we speak.

He that falls by himself never cries.

If you speak the truth, better keep a foot in the stirrup.

Man is harder than iron, stronger than stone, and more fragile than a rose.

No camel route is long with good company.

The account of the donkey is different from that of the donkey-man.

Today's egg is better than tomorrow's hen.

Two captains will sink the ship.

Two water melons cannot be held under one arm.

Indian Sub-continent

ASSAM

Because it has no bone, the tongue says all sorts of things.

He who does not know how to dance declares the floor of the courtyard to be sloping.

HINDUSTAN

Dictators ride to and fro upon tigers which they dare not dismount.

INDIA

Call on God, but row away from the rocks.

Do not blame God for having created the tiger, but thank him for not having given it wings.

I have lanced many boils, but none pained like my own.

Pray one hour before going to war, two hours before going to sea, and three hours before getting married.

The sieve says to the needle, "you have a hole in your head."

The tree casts its shade upon all, even the woodcutter.

Those who hunt deer sometimes find tigers.

To lend is to buy a quarrel.

Saints fly only in the eyes of their disciples.

When an elephant is in trouble even a frog will kick him.

Keep five yards from a carriage, ten yards from a horse, and a hundred yards from an elephant. But the distance one should keep from a wicked man cannot be measured.

For one who drinks swill there is one to trim his moustache.

When a poor fellow got rich, he had an umbrella over his head at midnight.
(*A symbol of richness in past times was to have a servant hold an umbrella while the rich man rode in the sun. The new rich would flaunt their wealth by doing it at night when there is no need for it.*)

After this, that, and the other, the sons of Kunti did not rule.
(*This proverb is reserved for the repeatedly unlucky souls who never make it, however hard they might try.*)

The reputation lost for a betel nut cannot be regained by donating an elephant.

The fence itself grazed through the field.
(*Lawmakers often break the laws they help make.*)

One without worries can doze off in a market place.

It is like trying to make an idol of Ganesh (*the elephant god*) and ending up with his father.
(*Some people try and fix things and just make them worse.*)

A bandicoot is lovely to his parents and a mule is pretty to its mate.

In the wedding of the mad widow, one who has a meal is the clever one
(*Or... if you can find order in chaos, then good luck to you.*)

Living in water and being an enemy of the crocodile is not good.

If you need a job to be done, be prepared to fall at the feet of a donkey.

It is like circling Konkan to reach Mailar.
(*i.e. going about it in a completely round about way.*)

The harlot who could not dance said that the ground was uneven.
(*This proverb is for those who make feeble excuses to hide their weaknesses. It comes from a time when women of ill repute were expected to sing and dance to please their rich customers.*)

Life is a bridge. Cross over it, but build no house on it.

Seeing the peacock, the rooster spread his wings.
(*A jibe aimed at those who try to pass themselves off as having talent and beauty.*)

If a sinner enters the ocean the water only comes up to the knee.

A single blow of a blacksmith is equal to a hundred blows of a goldsmith.

Utter a thousand lies and perform a wedding.

A few underhand moves in the performance of a good deed is forgivable

To the mediocre, mediocrity appears great.

KASHMIR

Giving advice to a stupid man is like giving salt to a squirrel.

I bought the nettle, sowed the nettle, and then the nettle stung me.

Ignorance is the peace of life.

One and one are sometimes eleven.

One man can burn water, whereas another cannot even burn oil.

One man's beard is on fire, and another man warms his hands on it.

The gardener had not yet dug out the radish when the beggar held the alms-bowl in front of him.

Asia

BURMA

Sparrows who emulate peacocks are likely to break a thigh.

CHINA

Adding legs to the snake after you have finished drawing it.
(*Doing something that is totally unnecessary and spoiling what you have already done.*)

An ant may destroy a whole dam.
(*If a small problem is overlooked at first, it can eventually develop into a disaster. As ants multiply rapidly and make tunnels in the (earth) dam, eventually this will cause it to collapse.*)

Crows everywhere are equally black.
(*Bad people are bad no matter where you find them; because human nature never changes.*)

Like waiting for a rabbit to bump its head upon a tree in order to catch it.

A donkey's lips do not fit onto a horse's mouth.
(*A polite way of saying that something is totally irrelevant.*)

People dream different dreams while on the same bed.
(*Even the closest of people, such as husband and wife, will have different thoughts and desires; be careful about what you assume concerning even the people you know the best.*)

A fall into a ditch makes you wiser.
(*We learn from our misfortunes.*)

Well-shaped feet won't be harmed by badly made shoes.
(*If you have not done anything evil, then you don't have much to worry about.*)

You can fight a wolf with a flax stalk.
(*If your enemy believes your weapons are deadly, he may be frightened away, even though you know they are really inadequate.*)

Searching for the ass on its very back.
(*Looking for your glasses when they're on the end of your nose.*)

Wise is the man who has two loaves and sells one to buy a lily.

As rare as a flea on a bald head.

All crows are equally black.

Flowing water never goes bad; door hinges never gather termites.

Like a frog in a well, looking at the sky.
(*Having a very limited view of the world*)

Having your ears pierced just before the wedding.
(*Delaying something essential to the last moment.*)

You won't help shoots grow by pulling them.

The wise forget insults, as the ungrateful a kindness.

Man's heart is a snake that would swallow an elephant: it is never satisfied.

A bird does not sing because it has an answer. It sings because it has a song.

A crisis is an opportunity riding the dangerous wind.

A hasty man drinks his tea with a fork.

A person who says it cannot be done should not interrupt the man doing it.

A single untried popular remedy often throws the scientific doctor into hysterics.

A whitewashed crow soon shows black again.

An ignorant doctor is no better than a murderer.

Better a dinner of herbs than a stalled ox where hate is.

Better do a kindness near home than go far to burn incense.

Dangerous enemies will meet again in narrow streets.

Weasels often come and say "Happy New Year" to the chickens.

Do not use a hatchet to remove a fly from your friend's forehead.

Every day cannot be a feast of lanterns.

Four things come not back: the spoken word, the spent arrow, the past life, and the neglected opportunity.

Govern a family as you would cook a small fish—very gently.

He has too many lice to feel an itch.

He that has no money might as well be buried in a rice tub with his mouth sewn up.

Hold back some goods for a thousand days and you will be sure to sell at a profit.

I dreamed a thousand new paths. I woke and walked my old one.

In reviling, it is not necessary to prepare a preliminary draft.

It's your own lantern; don't poke holes in the paper.

Talk does not cook rice.

Man must be sharpened on man, like knife on stone.

Never do anything standing that you can do sitting, or anything sitting that you can do lying down.

Of all the thirty-six alternatives, running away is the best.

One cannot manage too many affairs; like pumpkins in water, one pops up while you try to hold down the other.

Slander cannot destroy an honest man: when the flood recedes the rock is there.

The beginning of wisdom is to call things by their right names.

Three simple shoemakers brainstorming will make a great statesman.

The Yangtze never runs backward; man recaptures not his youth.

JAPAN

Being lucky is like having a rice dumpling fly into your mouth.

Better to be a crystal and broken than a tile on the housetop.

Don't rejoice over him that goes, before you see him that comes.

If I peddle salt, it rains; if I peddle flour, the wind blows.

If you wish to learn the highest truths, begin with the alphabet.

Never trust a woman, even if she has borne you seven children.

Poverty is no sin, but it's highly inconvenient.

If you have too many boatmen, the boat will end up on the mountain top.

A good husband is healthy and absent.

A man in love mistakes a pimple for a dimple.

A pig used to dirt turns its nose up at rice.

Not all married women are wives.

Deceive the rich and powerful if you will, but don't insult them.

Don't stay long when the husband is not at home.

If a man be great, even his dog will wear a proud look.

If man has no tea in him, he is incapable of understanding truth and beauty.

If you understand everything, you must be misinformed.

Laughter is the hiccup of a fool.

Talk about things of tomorrow and the mice inside the ceiling laugh.

My son is my son till he gets a wife, but my daughter's my daughter all the days of her life.

Never rely on the glory of the morning or the smiles of your mother-in-law.

Never trust the advice of a man in difficulty.

Sleeping people can't fall down.

The reverse side also has a reverse side.

The smaller the margin, the greater the turnover.

The tongue is but three inches long, yet it can kill a man six feet high.

To wait for luck is the same as waiting for death.

Walls have ears, bottles have mouths.

We're fools whether we dance or not, so we might as well dance.

A bee to a crying face.
(*One misfortune after another.*)

A fool is cured only by dying.

A gold coin to a cat.
(*Pearls before swine.*)

A sutra in a horse's ear.
(*A sutra is a Buddhist prayer or teaching.*)

Even a Buddha will lose his composure if asked something too many times.

Even monkeys fall from trees.
(*Even experts can make mistakes.*)

Fear earthquakes, thunder, fires, and fathers.

If three women visit, expect noise.

Like a cat's forehead.
(*Said of a small room.*)

Poke around in a bush and a snake will come out.

Protect your head and don't worry about covering your bottom.
(*Be careful not to expose your weak point while attempting to protect your modesty.*)

KOREA

A kitchen knife cannot carve its own handle.

The bad plowman quarrels with his ox.

The fish wouldn't get into trouble if it kept its mouth shut.

You will hate a beautiful song if you sing it too often.

MALAYSIA

A crime leaves ripples like a water beetle, a trail like a snail, and a reek like a horse-mango.

A lost wife can be replaced, but a lost reputation means ruin.

An ox with long horns will be accused of butting, whether it's guilty or not.

Ants die in sugar.

Don't use an ax to embroider.

He can see a louse as far away as China but not the elephant on his nose.

Smack a tray of water and you get to wash your face.

The existence of the sea means the existence of pirates.

The turtle lays thousands of eggs without anyone knowing, but when the hen lays an egg the whole country is informed.

PHILIPPINES

She who cackles laid the egg.
(*That is, he who talks first is the guilty party.*)

The bitter melon is not yet cooked and the squash jumps in.
(*That is, who asked you to join in?*)

They who spit should be careful they don't spit on their own face.

THAILAND

A tree near the bank of the river.
(*A person with one foot in the grave.*)

Don't make the bamboo water containers before you see the river.

Drinking water under someone else's elbow.
(*Like playing second fiddle.*)

If you love your cow, tie it up. If you love your child, beat him.

In the town where people wink, you must also wink.

Riding an elephant to catch grasshoppers.

Running away from a tiger and into a crocodile.

Like teaching a crocodile to swim.

TIBET

If sand is poured in the donkey's ear, he will shake it out. If gold is poured into the donkey's ear, he will shake it out.
(*The ignorant cannot tell the difference between things that are valuable and things that have little value.*)

A rabbit cannot put his paws on the horns of a deer.
(*Unless, of course, the deer has fallen through a snowbank and the rabbit is still on top...*)

The Americas

AMERICAN

A tree never hits an automobile except in self defense.

An American will go to hell for a bag of coffee.

Honesty is like an icicle; if once it melts, that is the end of it.

If you can't ride two horses at once, you shouldn't be in the circus.

In politics, a man must learn to rise above principle.

Never be content with your lot. Try for a lot more.

Never trouble trouble till trouble troubles you.

Cemeteries are full of people who thought the world couldn't get along without them.

When pleasure interferes with business, give up business.

ARGENTINA

Children's love is like water in a basket.

If you have a tail of straw, then keep away from the fire.

BELIZE

Don't call the alligator a big-mouth till you have crossed the river.

CHILE

A husband at home is like a flea in your ear.

EL SALVADOR

He who goes to bed with a baby wakes up wet.

He who likes pork rinds sighs whenever he sees a pig.

The skinniest dog gets the fleas.

The sleeping shrimp gets carried away by the current.

GUYANA

Cat foot soft but he ah scratch bad.
(*The cat's paw is soft, but it can scratch badly.*)

Don't mind how bird vex, it can't vex with tree.
(*No matter how angry the bird gets, it's useless to get angry with the tree it lives in.*)

Every best friend get a next best friend.
(*Your best friends have best friends apart from you. So the secrets you tell only to your best friends will be passed on.*)

Every bush a man night time.
(*At night every bush seems like a lurking man.*)

If yuh finger get sore, nah tek am and throw way.
(*If your finger hurts, don't take it and throw it away. Don't disown relatives or friends if they behave badly.*)

If yuh eye nah see, yuh mouth nah must talk.

It nah good to shove yuh foot in every stocking.

If trousers say massah teef, yuh can't doubt am.
(*If the trousers say their owner is a thief, you can't doubt them. You have to take the word of someone who is in a position to know.*)

Lil boy nah climb ladder to turn big man.
(*A little boy cannot climb a ladder to become an adult.*)

Moon ah run till daylight ketch am.
(*A wrong-doer thinks he is getting away with it until he is caught.*)

Nah every big head get sense.
(*Not every big head is wise.*)

Only knife ah know whah in pumpkin belly.
(*Only adversity shows a person's true self.*)

Tongue nah gat teeth but he ah bite fuh true.
(*The tongue has no teeth, but it can assuredly bite. Words can hurt as surely as biting can.*)

Turtle can't walk if he nah push he head outa he shell.
(*You can't achieve anything without taking risks.*)

HAITI

If someone sweats for you, you change his shirt.

If work were good for you, the rich would leave none for the poor.

If you want your eggs hatched, sit on them yourself.

Ignorance doesn't kill you, but it does make you sweat a lot.

The donkey sweats so the horse can be decorated with lace.

The goat which has many owners will be left to die in the sun.

The pencil of God has no eraser.

When the cat's stomach is full, the rat's back is bitter.

JAMAICA

Mi come here fi drink milk, mi noh come here fi count cow.
(*I came here to drink milk, not to count the cows.*)

Every hoe ha dem stick a bush.
(*For a hoe of any size, there is a stick in the forest.*)

Chicken merry; hawk deh near.

(*Though the chicken is merry, the hawk is near.*)

Fire de a mus mus tail, him tink a cool breeze.

(*The rat's tail is on fire and he thinks there's a cool breeze. He has no idea of the danger he's in.*)

Trouble no set like rain.

(*Troubles don't set in as rain does.*)

If you saw what the river carried, you would never drink the water.

Make a friend when you don't need one.

MEXICO

A person born to be a flower pot will not go beyond the porch.

Bad weed never dies.

He's afraid of the corpse but uses his shroud to cover himself.

(*He criticizes someone while taking advantage of him.*)

I don't even believe in the peace of the grave any more.

(*That is, I don't trust anyone or anything any more.*)

NATIVE AMERICAN

It's impossible to awaken a man who is pretending to be asleep.
Navajo

Those who have one foot in the canoe, and one foot in the boat, are going to fall into the river.
Tuscarora

There is no death, only a change of worlds.
Duwamish

Beware of the man who does not talk, and the dog that does not bark.
Cheyenne

When a fox walks lame, the old rabbit jumps.
Oklahoma

A starving man will eat with the wolf.
Oklahoma

There is nothing as eloquent as a rattlesnake's tail.
Navajo

The one who tells the stories rules the world.
Hopi

The moon is not shamed by the barking of dogs.
We are all one child spinning through Mother Sky.
Shawnee

Man has responsibility, not power.
Tuscarora

Life is not separate from death. It only looks that way.
Blackfoot

If you see no reason for giving thanks, the fault lies in yourself.
Minquass

Walk lightly in the spring; Mother Earth is pregnant.
Kiowa

Do not judge your neighbor until you walk two moons in his moccasins.
Cheyenne

Don't let yesterday use up too much of today.
Cherokee

Force, no matter how concealed, creates resistance.
Lakota

The bird who has eaten cannot fly with the bird that is hungry.
Omaha

All plants are our brothers and sisters. They talk to us and if we listen, we can hear them.
Arapaho

Old age is not as honorable as death, but most people want it.
Crow

In age, talk; in childhood, tears.
Hopi

White men have too many chiefs.
Nez Perce

There are many good moccasin tracks along the trail of a straight arrow.
Sioux

ACKNOWLEDGMENTS

Many friends and colleagues have provided me with material for this book and discussed its meaning and significance. I'm especially grateful to my family: Sue, David and Blythe.

The following are among the many books and Websites consulted in the course of compiling the collection.

BOOKS

A Dictionary of Superstitions, Iona Opie and Moira Tatie, Oxford University Press 1989.

A Treasury of Essential Proverbs, Rodney Dale, Book Blocks, London 2003.

Dictionary of Phrase and Fable, Nigel Rees, Parragon Books, 1993.

Dictionary of Proverbs and Their Origins, Linda and Roger Flavell, Kyle Cathie Ltd, London 1993.

Irish Proverbs, Fionnuala Carson Williams, Sterling publishing Company, New York 2000.

Superstitions, Peter Lorie, Simon & Schuster, London 1992.

The Encyclopedia of Superstitions, E and M A Radford, revised by Christina Hole, Helicon Publishing, Oxford 1961.

The Penguin Dictionary of Proverbs, Rosalind Fergusson and Jonathan Law, Penguin Books, London 2000.

WEBSITES

African Proverbs, Sayings and Stories
www.afriprov.org/
Commonly Used Proverbs
www.famous-quotations.com
www.firstfoot.com
www.inside-mexico.com
www.irishabroad.com
http://italian.about.com
www.manythings.org/proverbs/
www.quotationspage.com
http://spanish.about.com
www.wikipedia.org
www.worldofquotes.com
Superstitions
www.oldsuperstitions.com/
River Customs and Stories
www.england-in-particular.info/rivercust.
Scary Superstitions
www.corsinet.com/trivia/scary
www.sacred-texts.com/index
Thiasos Olympikos
http://home.pon.net/rhinoceroslodge/thia-sos
Urban Legends
www.ulrc.com.au/HTML/Superstitions_Archive.asp
World Death Rituals
http://death.monstrous.com
Yahoo! directory
http://dir.yahoo.com/Society_and_Culture/Mythology_and_Folklore/Superstitions/